Routledge Library Editions

INDUSTRY AND THE STATE

ECONOMICS

Routledge Library Editions – Economics

INDUSTRIAL ECONOMICS
In 10 Volumes

INDUSTRY AND THE STATE

P SARGANT FLORENCE

Routledge
Taylor & Francis Group

LONDON AND NEW YORK

First published in 1957

Reprinted in 2003 by
Routledge
2 Park Square, Milton Park, Abingdon, Oxon, OX14 4RN

Transferred to Digital Printing 2007

Routledge is an imprint of the Taylor & Francis Group

The publishers have made every effort to contact authors/copyright holders
of the works reprinted in *Routledge Library Editions – Economics*. This has
not been possible in every case, however, and we would welcome
correspondence from those individuals/companies we have been unable to
trace.

These reprints are taken from original copies of each book. In many cases
the condition of these originals is not perfect. The publisher has gone to
great lengths to ensure the quality of these reprints, but wishes to point
out that certain characteristics of the original copies will, of necessity, be
apparent in reprints thereof.

British Library Cataloguing in Publication Data
A CIP catalogue record for this book
is available from the British Library

Industry and the State
ISBN 0-415-31349-X
ISBN 0-415-31344-9

Miniset: Industrial Economics

Series: Routledge Library Editions – Economics

INDUSTRY AND
THE STATE

by

P. SARGANT FLORENCE,
C.B.E., M.A., PH.D., (HON.) L.H.D.

EMERITUS PROFESSOR, AND SENIOR FELLOW
IN THE FACULTY OF COMMERCE AND SOCIAL
SCIENCE, UNIVERSITY OF BIRMINGHAM

Routledge
Taylor & Francis Group

LONDON AND NEW YORK

Routledge
2 Park Square, Milton Park, Abingdon, Oxon, OX14 4RN

First Published 1957

CONTENTS

LIST OF TABLES

7

INTRODUCTION

THE State today has so many points of contact with industry that no apology is required for a small text-book describing them as comprehensively as possible. This book, however, is not just an analytical catalogue of State-industry contacts, and certain guiding ideas are introduced to connect and explain the facts described. Here some apology is needed perhaps for flying in the face of recent pronouncements on the end of *laissez-faire*. The facts of the State's positive and negative relations to industry in Britain I have found easiest to interpret, even today, on the basis of continuing *laissez-faire* or, at least *"laissez collectives faire"*; and I have followed John Stuart Mill and Stanley Jevons in justifying the various types of deviation from *laissez-faire*, each on their own merits, as rational means towards aims now, but not all formerly, accepted by public opinion. These aims have not always been explicitly stated, and for the sake of simplicity I have perhaps overstressed the more obvious among them, such as stability, security and full employment, equality, efficiency and democracy. I have, however, not ignored aims less openly proclaimed such as helping the small business, amenity, or just national viability and coping with circumstances and crises. In devising the rational means towards the aims desired, so much in industry depends, indeed, on the adaptation of procedure to circumstances, that some detailed analysis of the circumstances of different industries has occasionally been necessary.

I wish to acknowledge permission from the *Indian Journal of Economics* to reprint most of Chapter VI, and to record my thanks to Professor G. D. H. Cole and Dr. Michael Beesley in reading the typescript and making valuable suggestions. I also owe a debt of gratitude to my secretary, Miss Rachel Lee, for converting a difficult manuscript into that typescript so efficiently.

CHAPTER I

ETHICS, SCIENCE AND ART OF STATE POLICY IN INDUSTRY

AN introductory chapter is required for any study which claims to be a scientific approach to State policy. Value-judgments are involved which are likely to cause some confusion in the roles of author and of subject.

The policy of the government of any State is a third step in a practical syllogism of which the first two steps are some ethical purpose or aim to be achieved, which can be written in the wishful optative mood, and some fact or knowledge of cause and effect, which can be written in the indicative mood.[1] Thus when the State passes a law or issues an order (in the imperative mood) that meat should not be exposed in shops, this policy follows from the knowledge that flies settling on food carry, or might carry, disease, and from the aim which can be written "Oh that disease were reduced!"

Where States are not altogether autocratic, State policy must be deliberate in the sense that some deliberation between separate persons or groups of persons precedes or accompanies the final decision on policy, and that in weighing courses of action or inaction one against another, social aims and value-judgments are disclosed. Though they may find one value-judgment rationally incompatible with one another (such as the sanctity of fly life and the health of meat-eaters), natural or social scientists, as such, do not pass judgment on ultimate values. But the social scientist must take account of the values and judgments of the people who form the subjects of his study. Where the value-judgment and optative moods of his subjects are openly disclosed or uttered, it is possible for the author to record the fact of this utterance in the indicative mood, without

[1]Florence, *Uplift in Economics*. (Title of American edition, *Sociology and Sin*), 1929.

11

thrusting forward his own values. No confusion should then arise unless the indicative statement contains words like "principle" or "function" that may refer, optatively, to what "ought to be" as well as, indicatively, to what is.

Quotability is particularly important where the judgments concerned are those of collective organizations, by which is meant the judgments of persons representative of large bodies of people with similar fairly comprehensive interests. Though the State cannot be said to make value-judgments, it is possible to quote in the indicative mood the judgment of the government, taken to mean the persons governing the State for the time being.

As human history proceeds judgments are to an increasing extent uttered and committed to writing, and the scientific historian is less and less under the necessity of "constructing" the aims and motives of his heroes, villains or neuters. They speak and write for themselves. During the nineteenth and twentieth centuries, moreover, the State governments of western societies have on the whole become more democratic and the voice of the majority of people accepted as the final judgment of value. Under these circumstances, where law is not just a result of tradition or the views of a few men, and where representative institutions allow the majority view to be effective in legislation, a definite "public opinion" is on record. Dicey early in his *Law and Public Opinion in England* declares "the beliefs or sentiments which, during the nineteenth century, have governed the development of the law have in strictness been public opinion, for they have been the wishes and ideas as to legislation held by the people of England, or to speak with more precision, by the majority of those citizens who have at a given moment taken an effective part in public life".

At the present time (1956) British public opinion has probably become more unanimous than ever before in its values and more decisive upon State policy. To influence State policy people are organized into political parties which are usually not backward in publishing statements or programmes, implicitly involving value-judgments, and sometimes explicitly announcing them. When these political parties have a large membership or influence a majority or near majority of votes, their main explicit or implicit value-judgments may be taken to constitute at least a part of public opinion. Occasionally (and possibly 1956 in Great Britain is one of these occasions) the policies of the major parties, claiming between them a vast majority of votes, will not disagree very widely. The views they hold in common may then be taken as "public opinion" with some certainty.

This study is not concerned with public opinion and the value-judgments and aims behind *all* State action, but only with what lies behind State policy towards industry. The essential activity of industry is that of producing goods and providing for producers of all types (workers, managers, owners) an income with which to buy and enjoy such of the goods (and services) as they want. Policy may be called industrial because it follows aims directly concerned with the activities of industry or because it follows other aims upon which industry may impinge.

In his *Wealth and Welfare*, published in 1912, Professor Pigou considered that the economic welfare of the community as a whole is likely to be augmented if causes are introduced which make for an increase in the aggregate size of the national income, make for an increase in the share of the relatively poor and make for great stability over time. Avoiding controversy about the meaning of economic welfare, one may say that an aggregate increase, more equality and more stability of income are results of industry which British public opinion in the twentieth century judges of value. They may be called economic or industrial aims. In the early years of the twentieth century equal distribution was stressed; in the inter-war period stability; after the second war maximum income from full employment and productivity per worker. A return to an earlier Victorian age is thus appearing today in the public esteem of progress in increasing "productivity" and the total of national income.

Economic and industrial aims have thus changed in nature and stress; but what has changed still more in industrial policy, is the part which public opinion assigns to the State in attempting to achieve any given aims. In so far as private enterprise fails, the State may be judged right to attempt, or help in attempting, their achievement.

Public opinion is concerned, however, with aims other than economic or industrial—aims which industry may well tend to obstruct. Health is considered beside wealth, safety beside more productive machines, amenities beside industrial efficiency, guns before butter, democratic procedure and the defence of the "small man" beside industrial progress. Compromise must often be effected between industrial and non-industrial aims and here, more than among industrial aims, public opinion has fluctuated and periodically changed emphasis, and has permanently, perhaps, changed trend in its value-judgments.

These fluctuations and trends during the last century and a half will be briefly traced in the next chapter, as far as they have left their mark on the present position. Public opinion is not formed in a vacuum, however, and we must appreciate the developments of industry, contemporary and inter-connected with these fluctuations and trends in public opinion. We are not tracing the history of ethical value-judgments but of the art with which they were applied politically. Some scientific analysis is essential of the industrial situation, and its changing patterns, on which the judgments were formed and to which the arts of statesmanship were applied.

Industry is a word used to connote narrower or wider fields of activity and occasionally, though not usually, a field so wide as to include all work exchanged for pay—the whole economic activity. More usually, and it is a definition to be used throughout this book, industry is confined to activities, apart from agriculture, resulting in products not services: mining, public utilities (gas, electrical and soon atomic energy, water), building and manufactures. Manufacturing consists of a very large number of separable industries—239 are distinguished in the State's standard classification—separable largely by reason of the separate factories in which they carry on and in many instances by characteristic size-of-factory and location patterns. But with continued technological progress and new capital investment, and in spite of sociological conventions and "lags", these distinctions are flexible. New industries arise while old industries coalesce, separate, or die out. An industry, however, remains an important entity for practical purposes and its definition not just an academic or bureaucratic exercise. State policy as we shall find leaves many problems to be settled, industry by industry, and must therefore keep abreast of industry by amendments to laws and delegation of powers to bodies conversant with and representative of "an" industry.

In the free-enterprise, capitalist world, industries are not co-ordinated one with another by any human planning and command, nor is any industry governed as a unit. Instead, there is a "market" mechanism of demand and supply actuated by the incentives and deterrents of prices and of profits and losses upon a number of firms owning one or more factories within the same, or sometimes, different industries. Decisions are made (including plans for integrating new activities) and commands are issued within the constituent firm or combine of firms, and not at higher levels. These decisions, mainly about what to make, how much, at what price and with what capital investment, involve risks or, more specifically, uncertainties. There is the financial possibility of a loss rather than a profit to the firm, since the consumer, particularly where he has a choice of competing firms, may not demand all the products of the firm at a price sufficient to cover fixed overhead costs. There is also the hazard to the worker of unemployment through redundancy when his employer has to cut production. Partly to diminish risks as well as to lower certain costs, firms have tended to become larger and (with increase of capital for technological development) to be governed by Joint Stock Company organization. Division of labour within the larger firms has produced parties with specialized functions: employers and workers; promoters, directors, managers and shareholders. Much State policy is concerned with party relations and the organization of parties, particularly workers into Trade Unions.

The defence of workers from their employers directly by Factory and Mines Acts, or, indirectly, by defending the Trade Unions, was in fact, as we shall see, a most important early exercise of the art of industrial policy by the State. But other industrial trends besides the possible exploitation of the workers also ran counter to public values, and these also appear as problems to be solved by some type of State policy, particularly if the trends form vicious circles. Some industrial trends may be judged not to be in the wrong direction but merely to be too fast or too slow. Other trends may be confined to certain industries, and in the chapters that follow attention will often have to be drawn to the technical and organizational characteristics of particular industries as offering grounds for differing State policies.

These modern trends and characteristics general to industry or particular to certain industries may, when disclosed by scientific inquiry and analysis, help the art and practice of State policy negatively, as well as positively. Analysis may indicate limits on the State's action. For instance, the fluidity and variety of industrial structure suggest the unwisdom of clamping down uniform conditions, such as one minimum wage applicable to all industries. Alternatively, the facts may disclose means to be used by the State in carrying out its policy. The growing organizations of employers and workers may be found useful for delegating responsibility by a process of devolution; and certainly the discovery of causal trains and vicious circles indicate the importance of methods of preventing consequences, judged as evil, by removing the causes.

The fact about industry perhaps most important in State policy is the comparatively low level and narrow section where industrial decisions are made. The value-judgments of public opinion are likely to differ considerably from those of the persons deciding the policy of firms in particular industries. Under private enterprise the decisions of one firm may be negatived by the decisions of others, often to the benefit of the consumer, whose demand (i.e. the wants for which he can pay) can then be acclaimed as sovereign. But competition is not inevitable and the State takes action in industry largely to bring industry into line with public opinion. How, and how successfully, the State has exercised its arts to achieve that aim is the main topic of this book.

CHAPTER II

FOURTEEN DECADES OF STATE POLICY IN INDUSTRY

§1. *A Chronology*

THE preceding chapter has discussed the two main elements in the policy of the State towards industry, the value-judgments of public opinion influencing State action, and the development of the nation's industrial structure. The present chapter attempts to trace the gradual application of public value-judgments through State policy to the industrial situation developed and developing in modern Britain.

The simplest plan is to start by listing historical events in a chronological table. Two parallel columns are used: the main influences forming public opinion on industrial policy appear in one column, so far as particular dated events can indicate these influences; dated instances of State action, such as the main legislation, judgments and orders affecting industry, appear in the parallel column. To give some measure of the relative speed with which events unfolded, horizontal lines are drawn across the vertical columns to mark each decade from 1830 onwards. By 1817 the long Napoleonic War and its aftermath had ended and the date forms a convenient start for peaceful, post-war developments.

To trace public opinion in the first column the events that are pin-pointed are of three kinds. First and foremost the advent to power of statesmen, of governments and of types of civil servants able and willing to carry through industrial policy and legislation; secondly, events determining who shall form effective public opinion able directly to influence legislation by electing legislators—the Reform Acts are clearly indicated. These formal events will only take effect, however, if there is some pervading climate of public opinion in which statesmen and electors live and move. This climate is created by philosophers

17

and popular writers or speakers, by economic and political circumstances (such as wars, changes in birth or death rates, industrial developments and trade depressions) and by the organized mobilization of opinion. Not all these determinants of social climate can be dated; the industrial developments considered in the previous chapter are long period phenomena. But the first column can include the publication of climate-forming books and of official investigations, wars affecting social outlook and policy and certain agitations, *ad hoc*, or organized fairly permanently; in short, dateable external hot, and internal cold wars. In democracies where free speech is allowed, popular agitation may be conceived as one stage in legislative procedure; and the words and writing of individuals, such as Adam Smith and Bentham perhaps as yet an earlier stage in the "procedure". Certainly, as Dicey has pointed out, one step in legislation may form part of a "chain-reaction" (as we should say today) to help forward another step in the same direction; and—a process still better known—certain interpretations of the law, such as the Osborne and Taff Vale judgments, may force references back to further clarifying legislation.

In seeking trains of causation it must not, of course, be assumed that later events were caused by earlier events, *post hoc* does not necessarily mean *propter hoc*. But the chronological table may indicate as hypotheses plausible connections. The table should be read not only horizontally across, to detect the influence of opinion or of power-positions upon contemporary State policy, and diagonally downwards to detect the lag between the two; but also vertically downwards in the same column, to detect the effect of opinion and power upon subsequent opinion and power and the effect of legislation and its judicial interpretation upon subsequent legislation. Legislation usually affects subsequent legislation not mechanically, however, but through the crystallization of opinion or the modification of opinion after experiencing the practical result. In other words, the train of causation, if any, from one act of State to another, must as a rule be traced not directly downwards in the second column but in a zig-zag by intermediate reference to the influences eligible for the first column.

The chronology is intended to mark the visible high lights

in the changes of public opinion during the last hundred or hundred and fifty years, leading up to the present public attitude. These changes have occurred on three levels carrying further the distinction made in the last chapter between ethical aim and practical arts and policies: changes in the ultimate aims which society sets out to achieve; changes in the scope of activities assigned to the various agencies by which the aim is to be achieved, particularly whether by the State government—central or local —or by private organization and individual persons; and finally changes in the precise and detailed "devices" to be used by those agencies.

For example Harcourt introduced in his 1894 budget the progressive, graduated, principle in death duties which at intervals cuts down the capital of many an industrial firm. His aim was the more equal distribution of wealth. This had not been thought a necessarily desirable aim by the public opinion of fifty years earlier. Harcourt admitted as much by declaring in Parliament some years earlier than his budget that "we are all socialists now". The remark was intended as a joke,[1] but had an element of real meaning. When in 1909 on the other hand, State labour exchanges were introduced by (the then) Mr. Winston Churchill, no new aim was involved. Public opinion had always considered mobility of labour necessary for increasing economic wealth and the question at issue was only whether the State should function at all in the mechanism for mobilization. Labour exchanges were mainly a new means or policy for the end or aim of increasing national income. Delving further into means, when in 1944 Mr. Churchill's Coalition government passed the Distribution of Industry Act it had already been agreed by public opinion that a high and stable employment was a desirable aim and also, as the 1935 Special Areas Act indicated, that the State should act in achieving this aim. What was new was devising particular, subsidiary means of carrying out this government activity, such as endowing the Board of Trade with powers to build factories.

The term State policy is used to include both action enlarging the scope of State government and "sub-action" to adopt devices, once State government is agreed upon. These

[1]Trevelyan, *British History in the 19th Century*, 1923, p. 402.

TABLE 1: A CHRONOLOGY OF STATE ACTION IN INDUSTRY

	CONTRIBUTORY EVENTS	MAIN INDUSTRIAL LEGISLATION AND INTERPRETATION (Industry covers Manufacture, Mining, Building and Public Utilities.)
	1776 Adam Smith's *Wealth o Nations* 1789 Jeremy Bentham's *Principles of Morals and Legislation* 1798 Malthus' *Essay on Population*	1801 Health and Morals Act (Pauper apprentices in Textiles) 1813–14 Repeal of Statute of Artificers
1819 to 1829	1817 Ricardo's *Principles of Political Economy and Taxation* 1819–24 Robert Owen at New Lanark 1824–5 Huskisson at Board of Trade	1819 No Employment of Children under 9 12 Hour Day for under 16 (Cotton Industry) 1824–5 Industrial Tariff Reductions 1824–5 Repeal of Combination Acts 1825 Repeal of Bubble Act (restricting Joint Stock Companies)
1830 to 1839	1830 Ten Hours Day Agitation 1832 Harriet Martineau's *Stories in Illustration of Political Economy* 1832 Great Reform Act 1833 Royal Commission on Factory Hours 1838 Municipal Corporation Act	1831 Truck Act (Consolidation) 1833 12 Hour Day (Textiles). No night-work for young persons under 18. Appointment of Factory Inspectors 1834 Poor Law Amendment Act. No relief in aid of wages
1840 to 1849	1841–6 Robert Peel Prime Minister 1842 Report of Royal Commission on Mines 1843 Thomas Carlyle's *Past and Present* 1848 John Stuart Mill's *Principles of Political Economy*	1842 Mines Act. No employment of women or children underground 1844 12 Hour Day and no Night-work for Women. Safety Provisions (Textiles) 1846 Repeal of the Corn Laws 1847 Statutory Companies Gas Works Clauses Act 1847 10 Hour Day for Women and Young Persons (Textiles)
1850 to 1859		1852 Industrial Provident Societies Act 1856 Limited Liability for Registered Companies
1860 to 1869	1862 John Ruskin's *Unto This Last* 1867 (2nd) Reform Act. Household Franchise in Boroughs 1868 First Trade Union Congress 1869 Reports of Royal Commission on Trade Unions	1862 Limited Liability Act 1867 10½ Hour Day. Non-Textiles. (All Women and Young Persons) 1869 Municipalization of Gas by Glasgow
1870 to 1879	1870 First Competitive Examination for the Home Civil Service 1876 Factory and Workshop Acts Consolidation Commission 1876–80 Birth rates start falling	1871 Trade Union Act 1872 Adulteration of Food and Drug Act 1874 Municipalization of Gas by Birmingham 1875 Commercial Gas Companies Act 1875 Combination (Conspiracy and Protection of Property Act) 1875 Public Health Act 1878 Factory Act (Consolidation) Workshops, Potteries, Iron and Steel

	CONTRIBUTORY EVENTS	MAIN INDUSTRIAL LEGISLATION AND INTERPRETATION (Industry covers Manufacture, Mining, Building and Public Utilities.)
1880 to 1889	1882 Stanley Jevons' *State in Relation to Labour* 1885 (3rd) Reform Act. (Household Franchise in Counties) 1889 *Fabian Essays*	1880 Employers' Liability 1883 Patents, Designs and Trade Marks Act
1890 to 1899	1894 Report of Royal Commission on Labour 1895 Joseph Chamberlain at Board of Trade	1894 Graduated Death Duties 1896 Conciliation Act 1897 Workmen's Compensation Act
1900 to 1909	1900 Labour Representation Committee 1905 Liberal Government 1906 Anti-Sweating League Agitation 1909 Reports of the Royal Commission on the Poor Law and the Unemployed	1901 Taff Vale Judgment 1902 Education Act (Technical Colleges) 1905 Unemployed Workmen Act 1906 Trades Disputes Act 1906 Workmen's Compensation (Industrial Diseases) 1908 Coal Mines Regulation Act (8 hour day for Men) 1909 Fair Wages Clauses. Trade Boards (Four Trades). Labour Exchanges. Town Planning Act. Osborne Judgment
1910 to 1919	1914-18 First World War 1915 Health of Munition Workers' Committee 1917 Whitley Committee Reports 1918 (4th) Reform Act. (Women Householders over 30) 1919 International Labour Office	1911 Health and Unemployment Insurance 1912 Coal Mines: Minimum Wage for Adult Men 1913 Trade Union Act 1915-17 Munitions of War Acts 1916 Industrial Welfare Clause 1918 Industrial Courts. Trade Boards (Extension) 1919 Coal Mines Act (7 hour day)
1920 to 1929	1921 Reorganization of Trade Union Council 1926 General Strike 1928 (5th) Reform Act (All women over 21)	1920 Unemployment Insurance (Extension) 1921 Safeguarding of Industries Act 1926 Electricity Supply Act 1926 Public Health Act (Smoke Abatement) Act 1926 Coal Mines (back to 8 hour day) 1927 Trade Disputes Act
1930 to 1939	1929-34 Great Industrial Depression 1931 Report of (Macmillan) Committee on Finance of Industry 1936 J. M. Keynes' *General Theory of Employment* 1938-40 (Barlow) Commission on Distribution of the Industrial Population	1930 Coal Mines Act (7½ Hour day; Output Quotas) 1932 Import Duties Act 1934 Unemployment Act (Assistance) 1934 Special Areas Act 1936 Public Health Act (Part III Offensive Trades) 1937 Factories Act (Consolidating)
1940 to 1949	1939-45 Second World War 1942 Beveridge Report on Social Insurance and Allied Services 1944 Report of (Cohen) Committee on Company Law 1945 Labour Government in power 1946-8 Industrial Working Parties. Sir Stafford Cripps at Board of Trade	1940 The Conditions of Employment and National Arbitration Order. Essential Works Order 1944 White Paper on High and Stable Employment 1944 Ministry of National Insurance 1944 Distribution of Industry Act

CONTRIBUTORY EVENTS		MAIN INDUSTRIAL LEGISLATION AND INTERPRETATION (Industry covers Manufacture, Mining, Building and Public Utilities.)	
1940 to 1949	1947 1948	1st Annual Economic Survey Anglo-American Productivity Teams	1945 1946	Wages Councils Act Coal Nationalization Repeal of Trade Disputes Act National Insurance Act Borrowing (Control and Guarantees) Act Electricity Nationalization Industrial Organization and Development Act Economic Planning Board
			1948	Companies Act (Consolidation) Monopolies and Restrictive Practices Act Gas Nationalization
			1949	Iron and Steel Nationalization
1950	1952	Conservative Government in Power	1951 1953	Industrial Disputes Order Iron and Steel De-nationalization
			1956	Restrictive Trade Practices Act

devices may indeed have further sub-devices to give them effect. For instance when the Board of Trade builds factories in development areas they may or may not be clustered in Trading Estates and these Trading Estates may be run by estate companies with or without State loans. In short, deliberate State policies form a series of means and sub-means at different levels to fulfil a series of ends and sub-ends at the next higher level. As we go down from level to level the means and policy of one level become the ends, aims or values of the next. This study will, however, concentrate mainly on the higher means and ends, particularly on the social "aims" which form the ultimate and topmost end, and on the question of the scope of the State government and the (topmost) means and policies taken in furthering that aim.

The chronological table thus includes events contributing towards, or legislation marking, new social aims, new scope for the State activity, and occasionally some new devices for fulfilling that activity such as factory building powers in 1944, or the factory inspectorate in 1833 or Trade Boards in 1909. The selection of legislation, judicial decisions and other entries for the chronological table was not *ad hoc* but, with few exceptions, reproduces the items to be found in the pages of any short history text-book. The few exceptions occur where there was no one outstanding Act but a series of Acts amounting in aggregate to quite an important development of State policy. The precise Act selected for dating may be somewhat arbitary, but it is better to list one example of the policy rather than to clutter up the list with every example, or to omit any example whatever. The course of the chronological sequence does not run smoothly. Some of the decades between the horizontal lines are more empty than others. The comparative emptiness is particularly evident in the two pairs of decades 1850–69 and 1880–99. The stretches most densely filled with legislation affecting industry appear connected (1) with Sir Robert Peel's Ministry in the 'forties and with contemporary and previous agitation and Royal Commissions, (2) with the legal establishment of Trade Unionism in 1871–5 and earlier reports and discussion on that head, and the 1867 grant of the vote to industrial workers, (3) with the Liberal government and various agitations and reports of commissions from 1906 to 1912, (4) with the Wars of 1914–18 and 1939–45 and their immediate aftermath and (5) with the Labour government of 1945–50.

This varying "density" of State legislation is important as marking turning or "bursting" points in public opinion or the industrial situation. But to discover the nature of the turn or the burst we must look into the kind of legislation passed, not just its density. Two main contrasting periods are usually distinguished in the era 1800–1950. The first, the period of *laissez-faire* falls mainly before the empty decades of 1850–69; the second, the period of collectivism after the empty decades of 1880–99.

§2 Laissez-Faire *and the Minimum of State Interference*
The prevailing climate of public opinion from 1825 to 1870 is characterized by Dicey as "individualism". If every person is in the main the best judge of his own happiness then "legislation should aim at the removal of all those restrictions on the free action of an individual which are not necessary for securing the like freedom on the part of his neighbour".[1] Many of these restrictions had been imposed by the State under the medieval belief in a "just price", in the wickedness of interest, and in a

[1]A. V. Dicey, *Law and Public Opinion in England*, p. 146.

man's fixed status in society; under the Tudor code of paternalistic government; or under Stuart and Hanoverian Mercantilism. So the liberation of the individual implied first a repeal of earlier legislation. State action, under the individualist dispensation, came to be described as one of "interference" with some sort of "natural" order, and the right policy of the State as no policy.

The State, it was always agreed, must defend itself against external enemies, and, internally, must police itself—preventing force and fraud and protecting persons, property and contracts; and for these purposes the State must have revenues, some raised coercively by taxation. But under the influence of Adam Smith, Jeremy Bentham and a host of popularizers like Harriet Martineau, the State's industrial policy was reduced to *laissez-faire*—literally (in the imperative mood) *let* the private individual *make what he likes*! This call to freedom for industrial (and commercial) enterprise was extended to freedom of contract. The role of the State was merely to "keep the ring" round industry, to let men compete and fight it out, and only to ensure that they did not break the rules—especially their freely negotiated contractual obligations.

This freedom of enterprise and contract, it was held, would result in the greatest wealth of the greatest number since, able to pursue his own interests, each individual would, through the market mechanism, act in the consumers' and the national interest. If supply, whether of commodities or labour, failed on the market to meet demand, the competition of the many consumers or employers would force up prices or wages and further supplies would thereby be stimulated to come upon the market. If, on the other hand, demand failed to meet supply, competition between the many producers or employees would lower prices or wages and supplies would be checked. The labour thus unemployed and the other resources by which the commodities were produced, would be diverted to satisfy more pressing demands.

Labour could form part of this "invisible hand"[1] demand and supply "equilibrium" only if its supply was readily produced or withheld. Even though children could be employed as young as

[1] Adam Smith, *Wealth of Nations*, 1776, Book IV, Chap. ii.

nine, supply depended upon (re)production some years back, and certainly was not adjustable from year to year. Moreover the total population was in fact tending to rise sharply in the period 1781–1820 owing to a fall in death rates, while birth rates remained fairly constant. In the four successive decades of this period the survival rates measured by the difference between births and deaths per thousand of population were 9·1, 10·4, 13·6 and 15·5. The large families resulting were (until the Poor Law Amendment Act of 1834) often subsidized by the parish authorities—the local State government. Though, after 1820, there were fluctuations, birth rates on the whole maintained their big lead over death rates until 1870. In 1860–70 the birth rate was still double its rate seven decades later. In vain had Malthus called upon labour to keep down its supply by postponing marriage as a "preventive" check. The State was powerless. "Nothing," wrote Harriet Martineau in her *Stories in Illustration of Political Economy*, which, as Dr. Fay says 'converted everybody except the poor for whom they were intended',[1] "can permanently affect the rate of wages which does not affect the proportion of population to capital. Legislative interference does not affect this proportion, and is therefore useless".[2] In the writings of economists an iron law of wages emerged which precluded all hope of rising standards of living and which made direct action to fix wages by the State appear particularly futile.

As the chronology illustrates, the scope of State action in achieving the aims set by public opinion was in the period 1825–70, reduced to a minimum. Moreover the national aims themselves were not the same as today. Industrial progress and the increase of total wealth was then in the forefront, but industrial stability, equality and democracy were less highly valued than today, if valued at all. Low and intermittent wages tended to be dismissed by a shrug of the shoulder, partly because the State was thought not to be able to do much about it, but partly also because high wages and a more equal distribution were not judged, by the richer, ruling class, to be of high national importance. Even after the Great Reform Act of 1832 the ruling class, as measured by the voters, excluded all town and country

[1] *Great Britain from Adam Smith to the Present Day*, 1928, p. 369.
[2] *op. cit.*, 1834, Vol. III, p. 135.

labourers. Before 1832, the House of Commons, as Paley boasted, "consisted of the most considerable land-holders and merchants of the Kingdom; the heads of the army, the navy, and the law, the occupiers of great offices in the State, together with many private individuals, eminent by their knowledge, eloquence or activity". Paley himself represented their philosophy. The author of *Evidences of Christianity*, ranked his "Reasons for Contentment addressed to the Labouring Part of the British Public" as first among his works. The argument runs as follows:

"Some of the necessities which poverty (if the condition of the labouring part of mankind must be so called) imposes, are not hardships but pleasures. Frugality itself is a pleasure. It is an exercise of attention and contrivance, which, whenever it is successful, produces satisfaction. The very care and forecast that are necessary to keep expenses and earnings upon a level form, when not embarrassed by too great difficulties, an agreeable engagement of the thoughts. This is lost amidst abundance. There is no pleasure in taking out of a large unmeasured fund. They who do that, and only that, are the mere conveyors of money from one hand to another."

So much for economic equality and the higher standard of living for the workers which loom so large among today's social aims. As for democracy, this was not admitted as an aim by British public opinion till far into the nineteenth century. The turning point occurred perhaps when the second Reform Bill gave, in 1867, the vote to the town worker. Mr. Gladstone, known later, after his Midlothian campaign, as the "People's William", was not converted till he had witnessed the heroic conduct of the Lancashire operatives during the cotton famine[1] caused by the American Civil War. Important industrial experiments have in recent years been tried by the State as an application of democratic procedure. In the first half of the nineteenth century, however, the promotion of democracy was excluded not only from the activity of the State, but from the very aims that society set itself.

How were these limited social aims, and the limited scope of the State in attaining those aims, translated into policy? The chronology shows up two aspects of *laissez-faire* between 1800

[1]Magnus, *Gladstone*, 1954, p. 164.

and 1880, one negative, the other positive. The negative aspect is the more familiar and is marked by a series of repeals of laws. Tariffs were repealed that protected the manufacturer from foreign competition and raised prices against the consumer, notably while Huskisson was at the Board of Trade. Also repealed were Medieval or Tudor restrictions on terms of employment (many of which had already fallen into desuetude), such as the Statute of Artificers. The prohibition of out-relief in aid of wages contained in the Poor Law Amendment Act constituted a repeal of the "Speenhamland" practice. Though primarily an agricultural matter, the most famous repeal of all, that of the Corn Laws in 1846, must not be omitted since it was aimed at lowering food prices, and either raising real or lowering money wages in industry or a bit of both.

The disciples of Jeremy Bentham influenced State action from 1825 to 1870 so greatly that Dicey uses the "period of Benthamism" as a subtitle to the period of individualism; but as he shows, Bentham's thought was far from purely negative. Legislation was to become a science to promote the greatest happiness of the greatest number and the sphere of contract was to be extended into the "body of antiquated institutions" which presented, during the eighteenth century, a serious obstacle to the harmonious development of society. Moreover, in adding up for aggregate happiness, every man was to count for one and no man for more than one.[1] Thus Benthamism formed a bridge from eighteenth century "aristocratical" principles (where noble and gentle men counted for considerably more than one) to the full acceptance in the twentieth century of democratic State government, policy and procedure.

The positive aspects of Benthamite *laissez-faire* are clearly discernible in the chronological table. The activity of the State in this period is usually described as that of merely "keeping the ring". To cover much of the legislation of this period, however, "keeping the ring", if that be the right phrase, must include first of all defining and redefining the rules of the ring like disallowing hits below the belt. Truck Acts, for instance, disallowed and ruled against payment of wages in the form of employers' merchandise. Keeping the ring must also include

[1] Dicey, *op. cit.*, pp. 150–58.

designing new types of permissible weapons or protective armour and even allowing new types of contestants to qualify for competing in the ring. In the very hey-day of *laissez-faire*, there was a positive build-up or "structuring" of private, voluntary associations to act, for industrial purposes, like the free individual person whom *laissez-faire* was "letting be". Jurisprudence admits "artificial persons" and as industry developed larger and larger units and groups of persons, they became legal entities endowed with perpetual succession, capable of holding property in their own right and of suing and being sued as a distinct person. Rules were laid down as to the liability and relation of the sub-groups of persons within the whole group, for instance the shareholders and the directors of joint stock companies. This legalizing of certain forms of voluntary association was compatible with *laissez-faire*, since the companies, or other bodies created, still fought in the ring and the State merely "umpired" the ordinary law of contract and property. If the artificial persons cheated in the ring they were dealt with like natural persons. The chronology can only show the culminating Acts of 1856-7, though restrictions on joint stock companies were repealed and limited liability of shareholders gradually introduced throughout the period of individualism. Moreover, special statutory companies were formed for gasworks (as they were for railways) and special industrial provident societies were created, with rules which fitted the co-operative societies. Freed in 1824-5 from many restrictions, the Trade Unions received in 1871 their Charter—a set of rules constituting them, as Cole puts it[1] "a quite peculiar kind of legally recognized association".

"Trade Unions had a right to sue and be sued in the Courts, so that they could proceed against defaulting officers for the recovery of funds. They could not be treated by the courts as criminal conspiracies or as bodies unworthy of the protection of the courts because they acted in 'restraint of trade'. But at the same time they were protected against certain types of action arising out of their legality [such as members suing the society for failure to pay promised benefits, or enforceability at law of collective agreements entered into on behalf of members] that might have had dangerous consequences."

[1]*An Introduction to Trade Unionism*, 1953, pp. 169-70.

The Trade Unions have, since 1868, met in an unbroken series of congresses and the Congress, with its Council reorganized in 1921, has become a powerful force in the State.

Though it has largely escaped observation and analysis, the creation or "structuring" of artificial persons, as industrial development appears to need them, must be counted an important activity of the State, in relation to industry. To allow for this activity the negative conception of the State's "keeping the ring *round*" industry must therefore be widened to include the more positive acts of setting *up* the contestant bodies. This activity, carried on through the extreme *laissez-faire* period, continues to the present time.

"Keeping the ring" by no means, however, explains all the activities of the early-Victorian State, even when its strict meaning of forcing persons to honour contracts and personal property rights, and to avoid force and fraud is extended to the creation of juristic contestants.

The most obvious exception is the series of Factory Acts. These Acts limited the freedom of employers and of certain classes of workers in settling the terms they could write into their contract of employment. Certain other persons could not be given and could not seek employment at all. These persons were at first children or young persons and the doctrine underlying *laissez-faire* was not really infringed, since it applied only to adult persons, "able to know their own interest". Children and adolescents, it was admitted, had in their own interest to be defended by the State. The very first Factory Act, that of 1801, indeed defended only pauper apprentices who were considered, virtually, special wards of the State.

On a strict interpretation, *laissez-faire* was not infringed in mines till the Acts of 1842, prohibiting altogether the employment below ground of adult women, and, in factories, till the Act of 1844, when adult women's working hours were limited. Some philosophers considered then—and a few even now—that an adult woman was unable to know her own interests. To them none of the Factory and Mines Acts till the Coal Mines Act of 1908, limiting the hours of adult men, were any exception to the rule of leaving those who knew their own interests best free to make their own contracts. But we need not split hairs. Many of the arguments, emotions and sentiments that carried the Factory Acts certainly ignored the theory of *laissez-faire*. Emotion and sentiment either carried the day, as we shall see, or it was argued that even if workers knew their interests and what was good for them they might be unable to get it by individual action, unaided by the State.

By mid-century, then, the passing of the Factory and Mines Act showed a deviation in public opinion away from *laissez-faire*. These Acts were the fore-runner of a whole series sharply defining a code of State policy towards labour. The deliberate reasons for this deviation will be examined in the next chapter.

Writing as early as 1905 Dicey describes the labour code as "the fruit of more than forty enactments extending over the greater part of the nineteenth century".[1] The long, slow extension of the Acts from cotton to all textile and then to non-textile factories, was due less to lack of public conviction than to the slow extension of the factory system itself. The application of mechanical power and the congregation of people "in large numbers and under necessity to remain the whole interval of time determined by the employer or by custom"[2] (two criteria of a "factory" calling for regulation), only prevailed gradually in the wool, metal, pottery and the other industries which were after cotton, so gradually brought into the code.

The Factory Acts though the most famous were not, however, the only deviation from the doctrine of *laissez-faire* and non-interference by the State. At least four other types of deviation can be observed in practice by 1850. Adult private individuals were not let alone to provide all the information, all the public utilities and works for peace and for war, and all the means of exchange and finance which the nation required.

Second to the Factory Acts, at least for the interests of labour, comes, perhaps, the publication by the State of official papers about industry and trade. Indeed, information collected officially about the working conditions of labour was often the immediate instrument pricking the bubble of *laissez-faire* speculation.

[1]*op. cit.*, p. 29.
[2]Jevons, *State in Relation to Labour*, Ed. 1910, p. 72.

"Observation of the facts showed by induction that deductive speculation had miscalculated. Select Committees of Parliament, Reports
of Inspectors and Public Health Officers, Statistical Blue Books and
Royal Commissions all pointed to abject poverty and low wages,
the ravages of disease, and working practices which shocked public
opinion. These State documents were the material on which Engels
and Marx based much of their indictment of the capitalist system;
in the index of Marx's *Das Kapital*, Vol. I, there are more references
to British Parliamentary Papers than to any other source of information."[1]

The chief manifestations of this information activity are
recorded in the first column of the chronological table as con-
tributory events, since publication of information so profoundly
influenced public opinion and consequent legislation and administrative action. Indeed, some of the "information" of Parliamentary committees was undoubtedly selected for its political
effect.

A third activity of the State, not allowed for by pure *laissez-
faire* and yet performed at this period, is the direct provision by
the State of certain works and utilities, or their regulation and
control.

Adam Smith allowed that among other duties:

"The . . . duty of the sovereign or commonwealth, is that of erecting
and maintaining those public institutions and those public works,
which though they may be in the highest degree advantageous to a
great society, are, however, of such a nature, that the profit could
never repay the expense to any individual, or small number of individuals; and which it, therefore, cannot be expected that any individual,
or small number of individuals, should erect or maintain."[2]

These public works, such as roads, posts and other means of
transport are mainly auxiliary to industry rather than industry
"proper" as defined earlier, but the action of the State instituting
a penny post in 1840 and requiring Parliamentary trains charging
a penny a mile in 1844, all formed precedents for more drastic
action of the same type later. Gas was first manufactured in

[1]Florence, *Labour*, Hutchinson's University Library, 1949, p. 184.
[2]*Wealth of Nations*, V, Chap. i, Part III.

1801, and though statutory private companies were the rule, its manufacture was in a few cities directly undertaken by public authorities—the Manchester Police Commissioners as early as 1817 and the Corporation of Glasgow in 1869. Statutory Gas companies were regulated to defend the consumer against exploitation by the Gasworks Clauses Act of 1847; and the Commercial Gas Companies Act of 1875 inaugurated a sliding scale system whereby surplus profit was by profit sharing and price reduction to be distributed to workers and consumers.

A fourth, and perhaps the least noticed of the activities of the State beyond keeping the ring, was its role as consumer or purchaser of the products of industry. During the Napoleonic War the State consumed vast quantities of munitions and to some extent set a pattern of uniform large-scale demand which industry could meet with large-scale, standardized production. In the peace that followed there was still a constant though smaller State demand for ships and ship-repairing, victuals, munitions and uniforms, hospital supplies. Some part of these military needs were met by contracting to purchase from private suppliers. Another part, however, was met in the State's own arsenals or shipyards, thus keeping a nucleus of what we now call a "nationalized sector" of industry. But the State was, of course, seldom producing as a monopolist, or buying industrial products as a "monopsonist."

Successive Bank Acts and suspensions of the Bank of England's legal obligations to pay cash, bear witness to the fact that a fifth activity which the State performed, and was implicitly expected to perform, was general control over the whole economy to keep it on an even keel. As Court points out,[1] however, the aim was "financial stability and a balanced external account" rather than stable employment or "any responsibility for the employment of the national resources". Indeed, State policy "placing the emphasis as it did on the need to maintain an exchange rate fixed by the price of gold and to protect the gold reserve of the country, exposed the national economy to periodical bouts of severe deflation, accompanied by unemployment".

To sum up. Though in theory *laissez-faire* limited the State

[1] *A Concise Economic History of Britain*, 1954, pp. 120 and 192.

to "keeping the ring" around industry, policy as really practiced at the mid-century period of minimum State interference involved a much wider scope of State activity. State protection of property was always taken for granted by the then ruling propertied class. In addition, the State set up and legalized the contestants in the ring, began specifically to protect adults from overwork in industry, published information about industry and provided some of the public works, some of the demands, and some financial stability in the market. Much of State interference in the next period, was therefore merely a development of activities existing already, in at least a rudimentary form. Other State activities of the next period were, however, based on new conceptions by public opinion of the aims of society or of the role of the State in achieving aims old and new.

§3 *Philosophical Reconsideration*

The change in public opinion from the belief in *laissez-faire* and the minimum State interference was not initiated by philosophers. First came an emotional reaction to the facts and events disclosed in the industrial world which the State had "let alone". The information which the State published and the observation of residents and visitors in the new industrial towns—revelations which *laissez-faire* true to its principles freely allowed—spread horror and dismay. The greatest happiness of the greatest number did not seem to be working out. In the coal mines carriages were "sometimes drawn by children and women, harnessed like dogs in a go-cart and moving like dogs on all fours".

Facts like this, particularly when illustrated, as in the Mines Report of 1842, by sketches made on the spot, touched members of Parliament's sense of pity. Further pictures of "men and women working together in the mines almost naked, under repulsive and degrading conditions outraged the sense of decency of the House of Commons even more".[1] The enactment of the Coal Mines bill, altogether excluding women and children from working underground in mines, followed the report of the Royal Commission within the year.

Other legislation lagged longer behind the revelation of

[1] J. L. and B. Hammond, *Lord Shaftesbury*, 1923, pp. 71, 73.

B

the facts. Those who read government reports, even without pictures to help them, continued to be horrified. McCulloch, *laissez-faire* economist though he was, wrote frankly: "I look upon the facts disclosed in the late Report as most disgraceful to the Nation; and I confess that until I had read it I could not have conceived it possible that such enormities were committed."[1] But the bulk of men forming public opinion "before conceiving it possible" and acting on that conception needed the fire and compelling words of a Carlyle. As Carlyle himself maintained "we have looked into various statistic works, Statistic-Society Reports, Poor-Law Reports, Reports and Pamphlets not a few, with a sedulous eye to this question of the Working Classes and their general condition in England; we grieve to say with as good as no result whatever . . . Tables are like cobwebs . . . ; beautifully reticulated, orderly to look upon, but which will hold no conclusion".[2]

"The first revolt," wrote Sidney Webb in his contribution to the *Fabian Essays*:[3] "came from the artistic side. The first man who really made a dent in the individualist shield was Carlyle, who knew how to compel men to listen to him." It was he who spoke of political economy as the "dismal science" and who, as early as 1839, summed up its hopeless attitude in England's "infinite sea of troubles". "Nothing whatever can be done in it by man, who has simply to sit still, and look wistfully to 'time and general laws': and thereupon, without so much as recommending suicide, coldly takes its leave of us."[4]

In 1843 Carlyle drew attention to the kind of person *laissez-faire* left in charge and considered that "a government of the under classes by the upper classes on a principle of let alone is no longer possible in England in these days. . . . In Industrial Fighters and Captains is there no nobleness discoverable? To them, alone of men, there shall forever be no blessedness but in swollen coffers? To see beauty, order, gratitude, loyal human hearts around them, shall be of no moment; to see fuliginous deformity, mutiny, hatred and despair, with the addition of half-a-million guineas, shall be better? . . . If so, I apprise the

---

[1]Dicey, *op. cit.*, pp. 221–2.   [3]*op. cit.* 1889, p. 46.
[2]*Chartism* (1839) Ed. 1858, p. 8.   [4]*Chartism*, p. 58.

Mill-owner and Millionaire, that he too must prepare for vanishing; that neither is *he* born to be of the sovereigns of this world; that he will have to be trampled and chained down in whatever terrible ways, and brass-collared safe, among the born thralls of this world!"[1]

First of all revelation of the facts; then the emotion and violence of commentators; then the reconsideration of doctrine by systematic philosophers in the light of the logic of events.

This reconsideration was embodied in John Stuart Mill's *Principles of Political Economy*, first published in 1848. In his *Autobiography*, Mill describes how he reached the "conviction that the true system (of political philosophy) was something much more complex and many-sided than I had previously had any idea of". Among the many influences "streaming in upon me" were Carlyle's early articles, "though for a long time I saw nothing in these (as my father saw nothing in them to the last) but insane rhapsody".[2] "It was only in proportion as I came to see the same truths through media more suited to my mental constitution that I recognized them in his writings: then, indeed, the wonderful power with which he put them forth made a deep impression upon me; but the good his writings did me, was not as philosophy to instruct, but as poetry to animate."

Carlyle and, in the next generation, Ruskin, continued to influence public opinion emotionally. Neither Carlyle nor Ruskin, however, had much to say constructively as to the role of the State in meeting the industrial horrors which they exposed and which the policy of *laissez-faire* had left untouched or had created itself. But the final "Book" of Mill's *Principles of Political Economy*, is headed "Of the Influences of Government" and its final chapter "Of the Grounds and Limits of the *Laissez-faire* or Non-interference Principle". The upshot is that "*Laissez-faire* is to be the 'general rule'—but liable to large exceptions".[3] This wording, given in Mill's table of contents, still represents, I believe, the main basis of British policy on industry, supported by public opinion. Exceptions have become "larger" and are now justified by new industrial developments and new aims and

[1]*Past and Present* (1843), Ed. 1858, p. 295.
[2]*op. cit.*, Ed. 1886, p. 161.
[3]*op. cit.*, p. 489.

experience and arguments, but unless a case can be made out and *laissez-faire* proved guilty, it remains true today that non-interference of the State with industry is *presumed* innocent and even praiseworthy. Modern illustrations of this proposition will recur throughout this book, notably when discussing national wages policy, arbitration, or the nationalization of industries. Many writers of recent times, however, do not accept this proposition, or at best give the impression that they do not accept it. Laski in his *Grammar of Politics*, published in 1925, declared[1] that "*laissez-faire* as a systematic principle ended with the outbreak of war in 1914", and Lord Keynes in 1926 published his Sidney Ball Lecture under the title of *The End of Laissez-faire*. Since then, however, Totalitarian State governments were set up abroad—governments which really did "end *laissez-faire*"—and public opinion in the remaining countries has learned to discriminate the basis of its own policy from that of fascist and communist policies.

John Stuart Mill's "presumptive" *laissez-faire* was thought out at a time when a theory of more or less absolute *laissez-faire* had had its innings, and its inadequacy had been proved by experience. Mill's considered judgment was thus not unenlightened by facts and his reasons for clinging basically to *laissez-faire*, as it seems public opinion still does today, are worth summing up.

Mill's first objection to government intervention lies in "the compulsory character of the intervention itself, as of the levy of funds to support it". His second objection is the liability of suppression of minority and individual rights. These are both objections to the coercive sanction; often, however, a necessary evil. His third objection is the over-burdening of the State machinery of government. "Every additional function undertaken by government, is a fresh occupation imposed upon a body already overcharged with duties." But as Mill admits[2] "these inconveniences . . . result much more from the bad organization of governments than from the extent or variety of the duties undertaken by them . . . there may be almost any amount of division of labour within the administrative body itself". As government organization improved in Britain this objection lost

[1] *op. cit.*, p. 489.
[2] *Principles of Political Economy*, ed. 1849, Vol. II, p. 513.

force. Mill's fourth objection was the superior efficiency of a private agency owing to the stronger interest in the work. But Mill himself in listing the large exceptions to his rules maintains[1] that where "individuals can only manage the concern by delegated agency . . . the so-called private management is, in point of fact, hardly better entitled to be called management by the persons interested than administration by a public officer". In an age where the Joint Stock Company is the dominating form of industrial control, this exception to a large extent cancels out Mill's own fourth objection to State interference.

Mill's fifth and final objection to State interference in industry is more substantial and sounds a most modern democratic note. It is the "importance of cultivating habits of collective action in the people".

"Even if the government could comprehend within itself, in each department, all the most eminent intellectual capacity and active talent of the nation, it would not be the less desirable that the conduct of a large portion of the affairs of society should be left in the hands of the persons immediately interested in them. The business of life is an essential part of the practical education of a people; without which, book and school instruction, though most necessary and salutary, does not suffice to qualify them for conduct, and for the adaptation of means to ends. Instruction is only one of the desiderata of mental improvement; another, almost as indispensable, is a vigorous exercise of the active energies; labour, contrivance, judgment, self-control: and the natural stimulus to these is the difficulties of life. . . . A people among whom there is no habit of spontaneous action for a collective interest, who look habitually to their government to command or prompt them in all matters of joint concern—who expect to have everything done for them, except what can be made an affair of mere habit and routine—have their faculties only half developed; their education is defective in one of its most important branches.

. . . There cannot be a combination of circumstances more dangerous to human welfare, than that in which intelligence and talent are maintained at a high standard within a governing corporation, but starved and discouraged outside the pale. . . . It is therefore of supreme importance that all classes of the community, down to the lowest, should have much to do for themselves; that as great a demand

[1] *op. cit.*, p. 530-1.

should be made upon their intelligence and virtue as it is in any respect equal to; that the government should not only leave as much as possible to their own faculties the conduct of whatever concerns themselves alone, but should suffer them, or rather encourage them, to manage as many as possible of their joint concerns by voluntary co-operation: since the discussion and management of collective interests is the great school of that public spirit, and the great source of that intelligence of public affairs, which are always regarded as the distinctive character of the public of free countries."[1]

Against these five objections to State interference in industry, Mill put forward six exceptions favouring State action. One of these exceptions, meeting the objection of the State's lack of interest in efficiency has already been considered, namely that much of an individual's concerns are now managed by delegated agency, for instance by Joint Stock Companies. A second and more obvious exception has also been discussed, the incapacity of some people, notably children, to judge their own interests in undertaking work. The consumer, even though adult, may also be an incompetent judge of his own interest. "The uncultivated," said Mill,[2] "cannot be competent judges of cultivation." This exception to *laissez-faire* can be and has been carried further than the matter of getting education and now covers the defence of scientifically ignorant consumers against producers of material goods like food and drugs. Adulteration Acts began to be passed in 1860 and were made effective in 1872 and 1875. A third exception arises where individuals can judge their own interests, but are "unable to give effect to it except by concert, which concert, again, cannot be effectual unless it receives validity and sanction from the law". Mill specifically cites hours of labour where a minority of men by offering to work longer hours would undercut a whole class of persons' deliberate collective opinion of their own interest in shorter hours. The other three out of the six exceptions are summed up by Mill himself. "Anything which it is desirable should be done, for the general interests of mankind or of future generations, or for the present interests of those members of the community who require external aid, but which *is not of a nature to remunerate individuals,*

[1]*op. cit.* pp. 576-8.
[2]*op. cit.* p. 550.

or associations for undertaking it, is in itself a suitable thing to be undertaken by government."[1]

Mill's exceptions to individualist *laissez-faire*: three arising from the imperfect capacity of individuals, their lack of judgment and need to delegate and act collectively in concert; three from the divergence of the present individual's interest from future and general social interest, will continually crop up in explaining and justifying State policy.

Some exceptions have lost force, mainly owing to the growth of voluntary collective action, more, perhaps, have gained force. But in the present period to which we now turn, *laissez-faire* still appears the presumptive rule of British policy, exceptions and deviations from which must be justified for some specific reason.

§4 *Towards Present Policy and Thought*

Exactly when the "present" phase in public opinion and consequent State policy can be said to begin is not a question that need exercise us. The gap in important industrial legislation between 1880 and 1896 has already been noticed and also Dicey's distinction between the period of individualism and that of collectivism. Court[2] finds evidence after 1880 that "a slow but deep transformation of the values by which men and women judged existing institutions and codes of behaviour and by which they framed their actions and lives was already removing society from its Victorian moorings before the 1914–18 war. The war simply and immensely accelerated that process".

"Many things contributed towards the transformation. They included the emancipation of women, the beginnings of family limitation, and the decline of the birth-rate after 1870, which was the product of important changes in contemporary thought and feeling. A complete picture of the alteration in current modes of life would have to take into account many other matters, not least the decline in the influence of organized religion. This began to make itself felt among educated men in the universities in the 1860's, but was apparent in far wider circles twenty and thirty years later. It had effects which cannot be ignored even by the economic historian. A kind of social Darwinism

[1] *op. cit.* p. 530 (my italics).
[2] *A Concise Economic History of Britain*, 1954, p. 270.

influenced social and economic thought in the age that followed the publication of *The Origin of Species* (1859) and *The Descent of Man* (1871), as Benthamism had passed current in intellectual circles many years before. If Socialism enjoyed the power of a new religion in the last quarter of the century, this was to some extent due to its success in filling the gap left in some lives by the decline of traditional belief."

Though the new thought led away from Benthamism and from *laissez-faire*, invisible-hand, individualism, and towards greater belief in man's power over man's welfare and greater activity of the State in industry, it did not, in Britain, result in any great strengthening of the direct coercive power of the collective State. Collectivism included that of voluntary institutions like the Trade Unions and employers' associations and the collective bargaining between them, often with State participation. Collectivism also took form in representative bodies specially created by the State for the delegation of its power, such as Wages Boards or Joint Advisory Councils.

The Conciliation Act of 1896 substituted the indirect rule of a State participating with voluntary collective organizations for the direct arbitration allowed by Acts of 1824 and 1867 which were dead letters. In the view of Flanders and Clegg, it is "the turning point in the attitude of the government to collective bargaining".[1] Oddly enough it was a Conservative government that passed this Act—an oddity that can be explained by the inclusion, in the Cabinet, of Joseph Chamberlain—a "radical" who, unlike Gladstone took account of the realities of large-scale industry and appreciated its emergent problems. It was an Act that proved the forerunner of a series of measures, in particular of the 1918 Industrial Courts Act, the 1940 National Arbitration Order, the 1951 Industrial Disputes Order—all calculated to reduce industrial strikes and to forward the smooth and efficient running of the industrial machine. The precise relation involved between State and Industry was that of participation of the State government *with* the two main parties in industry, workers organized in their Trade Unions and capitalist management also organized in their Employers Associations or Federations.

[1] *The System of Industrial Relations in Great Britain*, 1954, p. 273.

The year after the Conciliation Act, Joseph Chamberlain was the moving spirit in passing another new law—the Workmen's Compensation Act. This Act, writes Sir Frank Tillyard[1] introduced "an entirely new principle into English legislation".

". . . up to 1897 no workman injured at his work could claim damages from his employer successfully unless he could show that the injury was due to some negligence on the part of his employer or his employer's servants. In 1897 Parliament enacted a measure which, while it left the existing law standing, yet gave compensation for accidents without applying the test of negligence, and substituted for proof of the employer's negligence proof that personal injury by accident, arising out of and in the course of the employment had been caused to the workman seeking compensation."

With the advent to power of the Liberal Government in 1905, State action in industry was intensified and greatly widened in scope. Arbitration under the Conciliation Act was used more than three times as frequently in 1905-13 than in 1897-1905; and a spate of legislation appears in the chronological table. Much of this legislation has been called "socialistic" if not socialism itself and seemed to follow from Harcourt's "we are all Socialists now", uttered during the previous Liberal era. New aims were certainly adopted, but the form of State action to effect these aims remained largely an extension under new industrial circumstances of the exceptions made by John Stuart Mill; and most of his objections to State interference continued to be sustained.

The socialism which percolated into contemporary "Liberal" public opinion was due to wider knowledge of the facts and to an energetic agitation, and thus repeated the pattern in the process of carrying the Factory Acts two generations earlier. The facts of poverty, low wages, unemployment and under-employment were disclosed in Charles Booth's *Survey of the Life and Labour of the People in London*, appearing in 1891, and this type of survey was repeated with improvement in the tools of its social science, by Seebohm Rowntree at York in 1899. Among the fact-finders and agitators who influenced government "circles" were the Fabian Socialists, including Sidney

[1] *The Worker and the State*, 1922, p. 30.

B²

and, in particular, Beatrice Webb who had been one of Booth's investigators and became a member of the 1909 Royal Commission on the Poor Law. But the Fabians would have had little effect without the growing power of Labour organized in Trade Unions and, by 1906, in a political Labour Party composed of twenty-nine elected members of Parliament.

The Fabians' aim was greater equality of wealth through constitutional action by a democratic State. In the original preface to the *Fabian Essays*, published in 1889, Bernard Shaw had declared for "vesting the organization of industry and the material of production in a State identified with the whole people by complete Democracy". Nationalization was in fact only carried out systematically fifty years later, but the characteristic twist was now given to State policy of looking to the details of industrial organization, as a material factor in the unequal distribution of wealth, and yet exercising the direct coercive powers of the State over industry as little as possible. Instead of extending the Factory Act procedure to other fields, the State came to rely on delegated powers and participation with voluntary industrial organizations, or on offering, for particular purposes, services and facilities like labour exchanges or technical education which workers could "take or leave". Mill had distinguished between two kinds of intervention by the government: authoritative, controlling the free agency of individuals, and unauthoritative, "of which so important use might be made". Evolving industrial circumstances were providing organizations *with* which the State could participate without coercion, for such detailed industrial purposes as industrial peace, mobility of labour, factory welfare, industrial rationalization and efficiency. These new organizations, were the large-scale Trade Unions and large-scale industrial companies, combines and trade associations.

With the new interest in democracy and equality it was realized that the human organization and control of industrial production had an importance of their own. To direct State interference in defence of women and children *from* industry was now added State participation *with* industry, State services *for* industry and State insurance *against* the risks of industry.

The first step was to break up the Poor Law and separate off industrially-caused poverty from other forms and to tackle that type of cause by industrial measures to be specifically justified. Poverty on account of the low wages of the able-bodied was to be tackled by Trade Boards—in those industries where wages were unduly low. These boards were to enforce a legal minimum wage as part of a national "standard minimum of the conditions of civilized life below which in the interests of the whole, no individual shall be permitted to fall".[1] Poverty on account of the unemployment of the able-bodied was to be tackled by technical education, labour exchanges and "to meet the periodically recurrent general depressions of Trade" by a ten-year plan of public works.[2] This new employment policy was embodied in the Minority Report of the Poor Law Commission signed by Beatrice Webb and three others, and the minority differed sharply from the majority report in regarding the low incomes of the destitute as the product of social conditions—of a vicious circle of poverty breeding poverty, rather than of personal responsibility and failure. It is difficult to realize today what misplaced humour Bernard Shaw's "what is wrong with the poor is their poverty" seemed to the Victorians. Even as late as 1907 it could be stated by the editor of the then leading weekly, that those of the poor "whose indigence had not been produced by their own fault" were "comparatively few in number".[3]

It was thus a new aim for the State to prevent the specific industrial causes of poverty which so often started workers round the vicious circle, or as the Webbs put it, down the "slippery slope", instead of merely picking them up at the bottom. The poverty due to low wages in industry or due to unemployment or other industrial mishaps such as accidents or sickness was to be dealt with separately by special legislation.

The treatment finally enacted was in fact separate and specialized, though not always taking the precise form advocated by the Webbs. In 1905 the Unemployed Workmen Act had allowed relief works at wages to be undertaken by public authorities, and in 1909 the Trade Boards Act created bodies to fix minimum wages in four "sweated" industries, while Labour

[1]Preface by Mrs. Sidney Webb to the *Case for the National Minimum*, 1913.
[2]*Royal Commission on the Poor Laws*, Vol. III, pp. 686-7.
[3]Quoted in Barbara Wootton, *The Social Foundations of Wage Policy*, 1954, p. 184.

Exchanges were opened to find work for the unemployed more easily. In 1911 National Insurance was initiated against sickness and, in selected trades, against unemployment. In these Acts the relation of the State to industry was not directly coercive; it was either to offer services or, if coercive, to participate in voluntary organization as on Trade Boards, or with Friendly Societies in Health Insurance. Except for the legal maximum hours and minimum wage for Coal Mines, enacted in 1908 and 1912, power was devolved or joint.

By 1912 the Liberal spate of legislation directly affecting industry seemed to have spent its force, and a popular reaction set in towards what was known as "direct action", by-passing the State. On the one hand the Trade Unions, whose total membership rose from nearly two millions to nearly four millions in the eight years 1905–13, staged large strikes and took on a Syndicalist ideology. On the other hand, the large-scale "Model Employer" like Robert Owen almost a century earlier, was again brought to public notice.

Syndicalism advocated the control of industry by the workers themselves, eliminating the State. Similarly, eschewing State action, a body of opinion hoped the bulk of employers would at last be enlightened enough to see that good works paid. Economists like Marshall, and Pigou, wrote of the possibilities of economic chivalry,[1] and Pigou quoted Marshall's last lecture as a professor in Cambridge to the effect that "The British Factory Acts are a standing disgrace to the country". The disgrace lay not in their character, but in the need for their existence. Much of the reaction to State legislation proved wistful thinking; doubt soon arose on Trade Union leaders' ability to manage industry, while chivalry appeared to be confined to so very few "model" employers. Yet the reaction halted State policy. No further direct State coercion beyond the Mines Act was advocated by the Labour movement for the restriction of men's hours.

With large strikes in 1910, 1911 and 1912 and mutual ill-will, "he would have been a bold prophet," writes Professor Court,[2] "who had guessed, in 1914 the uneasy combination of

[1]*See* Alfred Marshall, *Economic Journal*, 1901; Pigou *Essays in Applied Economics*, No. II, written in 1913.
[2]*A Concise Economic History of Britain*, 1954, p. 291.

trade unions, employers' associations and the State, by which industry has since come to be governed." Circumstances, however, again intervened. A desperately fought World War required an all-out national effort and put an end to any hope of achieving national aims by workers' or by employers' action alone. The coercive powers of the State were reinforced, and also its economic power as a producer of munitions, or alternatively as a customer and large-scale contractor for private munition production. State policy during and just after the war was, however, not confined to stimulating the production of munitions and controlling labour turnover and industrial disputes, but made both paternalistic and democractic attempts to change the social conditions of work. The idea of workers' control and employers' chivalry did more in the long run than halt legislation. The war-time State did not act entirely bureaucratically and single-handed. The ever more powerful workers' Trade Unions and Employers' Federations and Trade Associations were taken into consultation and began to participate *with* the State government in industrial decisions. At the lower levels of the factory floor, welfare work became a concern of the State and the Whitley Committee recommended joint works councils of employers' and workers' representatives. But a recommendation more extensively carried out was to set up Joint Industrial Councils at the level of a whole industry.

The war had been fought to make the world safe for democracy and the political vote was extended to include women in 1918 and 1928. In the same decade, however, deflation and attempts to return to economic "normalcy" were marked by a general strike and by Coal Mines and Trade Disputes Acts less generous of State help to Labour.

But circumstances again proved too strong for *laissez-faire*. The development of electricity supply needed for full efficiency large-scale central operation, and by an Act of 1926 a national grid was constructed under the control of a Central Electricity Board to wholesale supplies to municipal and private enterprises. Of wider import, a world depression, starting in 1929 brought unprecedented rates of unemployment, and led to political demands for State intervention—demands now measured by the votes of everyone over twenty-one. A general tariff was reintroduced after nearly a century in the 1932 Import Duties Act. In 1933 unemployment touched a rate as high as 24 per cent for industry as a whole, and when, in 1936, Keynes published his *General Theory of Employment*, a cry for general economic planning began to excite public opinion. Unlike the contemporary Five Year Plans of the Russian Economy, most British planners confined their aim to the prevention of unemployment. Even within this limited scope, however, the Government's response prior to the Second World War avoided the general stimulation of industry and consisted only in changing the rules for Assistance to the unemployed and, by the Special Areas Act, facilitating mobility away from the depressed areas and improving employment in those areas by economic incentives or at least hortatives. Most of the improvement in these areas had to come from the location of new factories and thus, as the Royal Commission on the Distribution of the Industrial Population recommended in 1940, the State eventually became involved in physical planning for employment. Previous to that, the State's physical planning had only concerned industry in defending citizens in the neighbourhood of industrial premises, under Public Health Acts, from industry's noxious effects.

The war of 1939–45 repeated and developed the experience and policies of the 1914–18 war. But no deflation was introduced after the second war and the shortages that persisted required the continuance of planning mainly in the form of controls over industry and over the distribution of its products. The advent to power, in 1945, of the Labour Party with its opposition to *laissez-faire*, and in particular its programme of nationalization of industries, added further to State intervention in industry and the density of entries in this decade of the chronology speaks eloquently of the new industrial activities of the State. These activities involved a wide variety of types of relation with industry, each of which will be detailed chapter by chapter.

To sum up the trend of the last five or six decades, new aims and values were developed by public opinion, particularly those of democracy and greater equality; and new circumstances arose, particularly the larger scale organization of workers and employers, the risk of massive unemployment in a market economy, and totalitarian wars. In pursuance of these aims, and to cope with these circumstances, the State became more active in industry, and often in partnership with industrial organizations planned certain tasks to achieve formulated aims. From the general policy of *laissez-faire* more and more deviations were made, taking the form of a wider and wider variety of relations between industry and the State.

Nevertheless these deviations remain exceptions which were justified by specific circumstances, specific arguments and specific aims. As against the ideology of totalitarian countries, British public opinion values the liberty of the individual as strongly as ever. Any action of the State towards industry which appears to threaten liberty has to be supported by assurances that curtailment of a business firm's economic liberty is no attack on individual personal liberty, and that freedom remains under planning. The industrial parties who are still "let do" are now collective organizations rather than individuals, but the burden of proof for its necessity still lies on State interference. The nature of this proof will be argued in the chapters that follow, dealing with the various relations of the State with industry.

These various relations must now be analysed. The State measures entered in the chronological table include all the main industrial laws, adjudications and pronouncements that are mentioned in shorter historical text-books. Our analysis, while comprehensive enough to provide some box or other for every entry, will be realistic, and will not provide any empty, purely theoretical box, into which no actual measures fit.

§5 *Analysis of Relations of the State to Industry*

Many books and pamphlets have been written about the aims and functions, or what ought to be the aims and functions of the State, in relation to industry. In this book the basic stress will not be on aims, or function (whatever function may mean), so much as on the precise relation between the State and industry in trying to fulfil social aims. A separate chapter will deal with each of the main relations.

The skeleton of a historical survey, provided in the chronological table, permits the reader to follow first the abandonment by the State of activities related to industry down to a certain minimum, and then the gradual resumption of old or assumption of new activities. The survey has proceeded far enough to enable us to draw up the scheme of analysis of present-day relations of the State to industry and to the parties in industry. Instead of speaking of various functions of the State we shall base this analysis on the fact that in its relations to industry the State government is dealing with sets of persons. Under the Factory Acts the State deals with one set of persons, the employers. In conciliation, mediation and arbitration on the other hand the State deals with and comes "between" two sets of persons: the employers and the workers, and all three work together, "participate", to avoid an industrial stoppage. The primary basis of analysis is therefore by the number and kind of parties the State deals with. The previous chapter directed attention to the separation in modern industry of employers and the multitude of workers employed in large factories or mines. Among Joint Stock Company employers there is a further split between promoters, managers, directors and holders of shares in the capital. In consequence of these divisions of work among different factors or agents of production the State has not only to "intervene" between industry as a whole and the consumers or citizens generally, but to intervene between the various agents within industry, the employer, the employed worker and possibly the inventor too; and between the various parties in the Joint Stock Company. These agents within industry and the parties in the whole modern economy may be briefly presented and grouped:

Capitalist Shareholder
Director, Manager and Promoter } Employer
Inventor   } Industry
Employed Worker

Intermediate, and Final Consumer
Neighbour, Citizen, etc.

The State, however, may not be "intervening" at all between agents and parties, but be a primary agent itself. In the nationalization of industry, the State-government takes the place of the employer and assumes a direct relation to the consumer, and to the worker. The framework of a realistic analysis now emerges within which the exposition of the State's relation to industry today may usefully fit.

FRAMEWORK OF ANALYSIS FOR FURTHER EXPOSITION

(a) *The State as a Third Party*

1. Keeping the ring ROUND contestants, and setting UP organizations as contestants (Combination and Trade Union Acts, Limited Liability, Statutory Companies., Employers' Liability; Company Law; "Trust-busting").

2. Defending one party FROM another.
  (i) Workers from employers (Factory and Mines Acts, Minimum Wage procedure);
  (ii) Consumers (and suppliers) from industry (Control of Monopoly);
  (iii) Neighbours from industrial nuisances (Public Health Acts; Town Planning);
  (iv) Shareholders from Promoters and Directors (Company Law);
  (v) Inventors from Pirates or Consumers from Inventors, (Patent Acts).

3. Participating WITH employers and workers. Devolution of Government (Conciliation Act; Industrial Courts; Industrial Organization and Development; Joint Advisory Bodies; Joint Industrial Councils).

(b) *The State as the Primary Party*

4. Publishing of information ABOUT industry.

5. Providing a palliative AGAINST industrial mishaps (Poor Law, Workmen's Compensation, Unemployment Insurance; Unemployed Workmen Act).

6. Providing a service FOR industry (Labour Exchanges; Technical Schools; Trading Estates; Scientific Research).

7. Operation OF particular industries (Nationalization, Municipal Trading).

8. Trading IN particular industries, e.g., Victualling, Housing (Fair Wages Clause).

(c) *The State as the Secondary Party*

9. Control OVER industry as such (not separate industrial parties) through various governmental bodies, towards certain aims (e.g. financial stability, full employment, equality, national viability) by various procedures: incentive and deterrent; coercive and physical. (Tariffs, subsidies, purchase taxes, profits taxes, budgetary policy and Bank Rate; rationing, allocations, licensing, direction of labour.)

A relation of one person or set of persons to another is expressed most simply by a preposition. The Oxford Concise Dictionary defines a preposition as a "word serving to mark relations between the noun or pronoun it governs and another word", and we may mark the different relations between State and Industry by distinctive prepositions. These operative prepositions, printed in capitals in the Analysis, are *round, up, from, with, about, against, for, of, in,* and *over.* The action of the State in keeping the ring round industry and setting up organizations has already been sufficiently discussed. Chapter IV will discuss the State defence of industrial parties from one another; Chapter V, State participation with industrial parties; Chapter VI, State information about, and services for, industry, and palliatives against the hazards of industry; Chapter VII, State operation of, and trading in, industries; Chapter VIII, State control over industry.

Each chapter will describe present legislation and State policies and, where significant, their procedure, timing and coverage related to the circumstances of industry in general or to the characteristics of the particular industries to which they apply. Whenever the aims of these policies were explicitly stated or can be gauged from public opinion we shall proceed to discuss the success of the policies adopted in achieving these aims.

CHAPTER III

STATE DEFENCE FROM EXPLOITATION

§1 *Direct Defence of Labour from the Employer*

THE classical case of protection by the State of one industrial party from another is the series of Factory and Mines Acts. They protect the workers from his employer in respect of working hours and physical conditions even to the extent of altogether prohibiting the employment of certain classes of persons. Our chronology shows that these Acts were the earliest form of this protective relation of the State to parties in modern industry. The form of the relation is simple, and all but recent trends are recounted in much detail by text-books. Nothing but a brief analysis of procedure and aims is needed to round out the history of the Acts given with the chronology.

The State legislature specifies (or gives the Minister power to order) certain maximum hours and minimum working conditions as a ceiling and a floor above and below which the employer may not go. For instance, women and young persons may not, under the latest consolidating Factory Act, 1937, be worked more than four and a half hours at a stretch and, normally, nine hours a day with one half-holiday, or forty-eight hours a week. To meet pressure of work, certain exceptional overtime is allowed, but not more than 6 hours in any of 25 weeks in the year or more than a total of 100 hours. No work is allowed on Sundays and six holidays in the year. Factory Acts also specify the permitted incidence of working hours, that is the actual times of day between which women and young persons may work; no nightwork, for instance, is permitted—a restriction which limits the application of multiple shifts.

In coal mining, Acts have fixed a maximum of working hours for men: 8 in 1908, 7 in 1919, back to 8 in 1926, 7½ in 1930. The definite deviation from *laissez-faire* in 1908 was a measure of the new power of Labour in the State. It is significant, however, that direct legislation for limiting men's hours has not been attempted in other industries. Though the Coal Mines Acts were the measure of a new power they were also the last extension of an old procedure. Men's Trade Unions have learned to appreciate their own strength and no longer ask for direct State protection of their hours of work by the Factory Act procedure.

By this procedure, applicable mainly to women and young persons, inspectors are appointed by ministries of the central Government. They have the right of entry into factories or mines and can prosecute the employers in the ordinary courts of justice for any infringement they may detect of the detailed law. On winning the case, the State can exact considerable fines. This system is direct, fully processed, coercive rule. The central Government makes the law and forces employers to obey by its executive action through the courts of justice.

The maximum hours made compulsory by the State are not however the actual hours worked. They form the ceiling below which a shorter maximum is agreed upon by collective bargaining with the Trade Unions (beyond which overtime rates will be paid), and often a still shorter actual period is worked, according to the policy of factory managements, usually in agreement with the factory workers. While the legal maximum weekly hours for women is 48, the actual hours they worked, on average, for all manufacturing industries was found in April and October 1953, and again in April 1954, to be 42.[1]

The aims of fixing a legal maximum of hours are greater leisure and health for the workers and preventing the exploitation of their energies generally. "The workers," said Winston Churchill, when introducing in 1908 the eight-hour bill for coal miners, "would no longer be content with an existence which condemned them day after day to go from bed to the mill, from the mill back to bed."[2] And with the increasing speeds of work and distances to journey from home to factory, the reasons for shorter hours grow stronger. Greater health is also aimed at by the Factory Acts' protection of all workers from poisons, dirt, overcrowding, excessive heat or cold, poor lighting, wet

[1] *Ministry of Labour Gazette*, Sept. 1954, p. 302.
[2] Halévy, *History of the English People*, 1905–1915, p. 239.

floors, dust and stagnant air. Sanitary conveniences, drinking water, washing facilities and accommodation for clothing must be provided (together with seating facilities), if women are employed. A further aim of the Factory and Mines Acts, where success is measurable in the steady reduction of accident rates (apart from times of war), is that of safety. Dangerous machinery must be fenced and protective clothing worn, young persons instructed before working certain machinery and a host of detailed regulations kept according to the type of industry, process, equipment and building.

Though the aims of this procedure, the greater health, safety and leisure of the workers and the prevention of their exploitation still exercises public opinion, the general procedure of the Factory and Mines Acts has not been extensively applied in the other and more recent preventive activities of the State. As we shall see, "indirect rule" through Boards representing workers and employers was adopted for fixing minimum wages, and trilateral participation of the State with workers' and employers' collective organizations has been the newer procedure, rather than direct unilateral State action.

Coercion direct by the State is, however, still adopted in one set of circumstances, namely where effective protection of the worker depends upon accurate scientific knowledge. The most efficient method of preventing occupational disease and the very question of whether a disease is occupational in origin, and many questions of safety, cannot be decided by majority vote among representatives. The answer can only be reached by experts and implementation of their views is achieved most simply by direct State government fiat. In the last fifty years scientific research has been extended from industrial physiology to industrial psychology and sociology, and experts have been employed to investigate the effects of various lengths, distribution and incidence, of hours, and of various incentives and social conditions upon productivity. During the First World War Lloyd George, as Minister of Munitions, set up a Health of Munition Workers Committee, which issued twenty-three reports. The most famous of these showed the inefficiency of twelve-hour and ten-hour working days as measured by lower output and a higher rate of absence and accidents. Similar

54 INDUSTRY AND THE STATE

results were obtained by the United States Public Health Service in their *Bulletin* 106 (issued in 1919), comparing a ten-hour and an eight-hour plant, and an eight-hour day or a forty-eight-hour week appeared as a probable optimum for efficiency in the long run.[1] These findings lent support not only to the Trade Unions' demand for a forty-eight-hour week (more or less fulfilled by 1919) but justified the 1937 Factory Acts' forty-eight-hour normal ceiling for women and young persons in all manufactures. With shorter hours established, industrial researches like that of Elton Mayo in America and of the Industrial Fatigue (later Health) Research Board (which succeeded the Health of Munition Workers Committee) in Britain turned to the psychological and social factors underlying efficiency and morale. These researches probably also influenced the State's coercive procedure. During the Second World War factories were by order required to appoint welfare officers and joint consultative bodies. But compulsory consultation is almost a contradiction in terms, and we hear more today of consultation than compulsion.

Scientific investigation may well upset preconceived notions. The protracted inquiries into hours of labour have, in my view for instance, failed to establish a case for the differential treatment of adult women. Provided that women workers have not double duties to perform as mothers or housewives on top of their industrial work, they seem no more subject to reduced health and efficiency owing to long hours of work than men. Legal reduction of women's hours has, of course, in most industries forced the reduction of men's hours, since men and women work side by side and organization would break down when the women leave. This consequence was quite realized by the early agitators for legal shorter hours for women only, and the men were accused of "hiding behind the women's petticoats". So, in fact, the Factory Acts served their turn in reducing the working hours of all workers when and wherever Trade Unions were still weak.

To sum up, workers know their interests in shorter hours, including holidays with pay, and with full employment only require to be organized to get them. Stronger trade unionism

[1]Florence, *Labour*. Hutchinson's University Library, 1949, pp. 51-8.

has, in short, reduced the need for Factory Acts. Compulsion by Factory Act remains now of greater use in scientifically modifying physical conditions whose effect on ill-health and accidents the worker cannot fully know or judge. In the defence from these hazards the provisions of the Acts may well be extended to other places besides Factories and Mines, where industry may be carried on dangerously. The Gowers committee of inquiry (Cmd. 7664) into health, welfare and safety in employment not covered by the Acts hailed the Factory Act of 1937 (p. 12) as "a model in its own field of what protective legislation can accomplish" and recommended a similar defence against similar physical hazards in shops, warehouses and offices. The British Factory Acts have also been widely copied in other countries especially those with weaker Trade Unions. A high proportion of the International Labour Office conventions ratified by member States are of this type.

§2 *The Wages Councils and Alternative Structures*

The Factory Acts, starting in 1801, defended women and young workers from employment, or employment at long hours, in conditions likely to injure their health and safety. The Trade Boards, starting over a century later, aimed to defend all workers—men as well as women—in certain trades from employment at low wages. At first, minimum wages only were considered, as a "floor" below which the standard for the normal worker must not fall; but, later, scales were fixed for different occupations and grades of workers within each industry and for overtime and piece-work—special rates were fixed too for learners and subnormal workers. The significant difference from the Factory Act procedure was that the exact minimum or other wage rates to be paid were not written into the Act as maximum hours had been, but were left to specially created structures, "Boards" or "Councils", for each of the industries selected.

The composition of these Boards or Councils consists of representatives of employers and workers in equal numbers and a smaller number of independent members usually three, one of whom is designated chairman. The numbers of representatives from each side is usually about ten to twenty, but varies greatly with the variety of interests to be included—some industries being more heterogeneous than others. Most of the representatives are nominees of employers' associations or the Trade Unions. As now stipulated, under the 1945 Wages Councils Act, all members are appointed by the Minister of Labour, but before the representatives are chosen the Minister must consult the appropriate workers', or employers', organization. In fact the organizations normally get the representative they want. Wages Councils now exist in many retail trades and in about 40 manufacturing industries, a few of which have separate councils for England and Scotland. Some large industries are involved such as baking, shoe repairing, dressmaking, tailoring, hollow-ware and laundries, but many of the industries like coffin furniture and cement making, the perambulator and the invalid carriage trade, employ but a small total of workers.

In nearly all the industries with Wages Councils small or medium sized factories prevail, rather than large. About half of all the industries where the majority of workers are in small plants (employing 100 or less) have Wages Councils. Among large or largish plant industries (with the majority of workers in factories employing over 500) only two rely for wage-fixing on Wages Councils alone: tin boxes and wholesale bespoke tailoring.

A still more significant characteristic of industries where Wages Councils have been applied is the high proportion of women employed. The average proportion of women to men employed in manufactures generally is about 1 to 2, but a majority of the Wages Council industries have the opposite situation—a ratio of women to men of 2 to 1 or more.

Factory Acts defend from long hours only women and young persons. The Wages Council procedure applied to all, but the Councils tend to be created mainly in those industries with women in the majority. Collective bargaining about wages without State interference is thus left mainly to the industries employing a large preponderance of men. The degree of State interference in the wage fixing of an industry appears, in short, to be correlated with the proportion of women that industry employs.

Though contact of the State with industry was thus more

indirect and cushioned by joint bodies than under the Factory Acts, the State government even under the Wages Councils procedure does impinge on industry at a number of points.[1]

(i) The Minister is empowered to establish Councils if he is of opinion that no adequate machinery exists for the effective regulation of the remuneration of the workers.

(ii) He makes a thorough inquiry into the industry before coming to this opinion.

(iii) The Minister appoints the representatives of both sides in consultation with them, and the independent members without consulting the industrial parties. Since the representative members usually cancel out, the independent nominated members tip the balance in making decisions.

(iv) Decisions of the Councils must be submitted to the Ministry of Labour and can be referred back. This is justified particularly by the danger that the set of wage-rates fixed by the Councils of different industries may be unco-ordinated and out of line one with another.

(v) The Ministry makes the Wages Regulation Order to give effect to the Councils' Proposals.

(vi) Inspectors are appointed by, and responsible to, the Minister; in 1954 a staff of nearly 200 investigated complaints and made routine inspections.

(vii) Infringement of the Councils' Regulations are brought up as criminal cases before the ordinary judicial authorities of the State. The coercive sanction actually applied is indicated by the average of £100,000, paid back by employers in arrears for each of the years 1951 and 1952. Legal proceedings were taken in eleven cases.

Tillyard sums up[2] that in the case of the Trade Boards (now Wages Councils), the control of the Ministry of Labour over their *legislation* is very slight, but that *administration* is not merely controlled by, but substantially vested in the Ministry. In short a real separation of powers as advocated by Montesquieu is practised, not just between separate organs of the State, but between the State and bodies with joint representation from voluntary collective organizations.

[1]Annual Reports of the Ministry of Labour, e.g. 1953, Cmd. 8893.
[2]*The Worker and the State*, 1922, p. 52.

In aiming to defend the workers' wage from employers' exploitation the State could have adopted methods alternative to the Wages Councils. The most direct procedure would have been to write a minimum wage into the Act either of universal application, or different for different industries or different regions. In the United States, for instance, under the Fair Labour Standards Act of 1938, after a period allowing for regional differentiation, a universally applicable minimum rate per hour of 40 cents was to be paid by the year 1945. In Britain this direct method was, in the Factory Acts, adopted for fixing hours and other conditions of work but was thought less suitable for fixing wages for at least five reasons.

(i) With inflation and deflation the purchasing power of money varies from year to year. The American 40 cents an hour became, in fact, completely obsolete in 1945. In these post-war days of inflation, a new Act would have to be put through the State legislature every year!

(ii) Setting limits to the hours of work and setting standards of physical environment in a factory are largely a matter of scientific knowledge about the ventilation, rest periods and so on, necessary for human beings generally, a knowledge which the State eminently possesses. But wages (though the source of a scientifically adequate or inadequate nutrition) are more remotely related to general scientific knowledge and far more a matter of compromise, taking into account not only basic needs for life but what each particular trade can bear.

(iii) The danger of repercussion and boomerang effects (for instance, on the level of unemployment) is more easily assessed industry by industry by a joint discussion between the employers, the employed and independent members.

(iv) With so many unknowns, an experimental or, in Jevons' words, "Baconian" approach is of advantage. A few Boards or Councils each confined to one industry can be observed as testing grounds before proceeding further.

(v) Even if other things were equal, there remain the arguments advanced so clearly by Mill for self-help and devolution rather than the autocratic fiat by Act or order of the central government.

Another alternative to the Wages Council methods is that of arbitration which has been tried, notably, in New Zealand and the Australian States and Commonwealth. Though the State does not exclusively fix the wage, as under the Wage-by-Act system, the State under the Wage-by-Arbitration procedure still plays a direct and major role. In some States employers or workers initiate the procedure by asking for the intervention of the Arbitration Court, but in others the parties are compelled to refer disputes to the Court. The Court consists of permanent State-appointed judges, and its procedure with lawyers formally pleading on one side and the other, generates the atmosphere of the arena. Once the Court makes its decision there is compulsion to submit to the award and to refrain from any efforts to alter it. Wages set by arbitration which might be supposed to result in a more logical level and structure of wages than wages set by a number of Councils or Boards has been rejected as British policy, largely because of the power it gives the State compared with the autonomy of interested parties. As the aims of the State policy have developed from correcting low wages to filling the gap in collective bargaining on wages, so arbitration has become a less suitable instrument. Public opinion has certainly moved nearer to Professor Eva Burns' contention twenty years ago.[1]

"If industrial peace ultimately depends upon the belief that any particular settlement is just, there is reason to believe that the Board System will prove more successful, in that it introduces a measure of self-government into industry. Under Arbitration the parties only meet when feeling is bad. The cause of meeting is the existence of a disagreement. This tends to give both the worst impression of each other and concentrates attention on the wages question as the only point of contact between them. But under the Board [now, Council] System it is possible to have a standing body which can act as the parliament of the industry. Such a body can deal with many other matters besides wages, and will meet not merely in times of stress. Many of the problems which a self-governing industry would have to solve require technical knowledge and inside information about the special needs of the trade. For such purposes a body of experts is preferable to an independent judge."

[1] *Wages and the State*, 1926, p. 245.

§3 *Aims of the Wages Councils*

Of the possible alternatives in State action on wages, the structure and procedure adopted in Britain was that of the Wages Councils. Questions that must now be answered are what were, or have become, the precise aims of these Councils or Boards; was State action, and this particular organization and relation of State and industry, necessary for the aim in view; how far has it in fact proved successful in achieving its aim without adverse repercussions; and is the system likely to be extended or modified in the future?

Under the Act of 1909 the first four Trade Boards were set up in industries where the rate of wages was "unduly" low. The Act permitted the Board of Trade to promote a provisional order to apply the provisions of the Act to other trades where rates of wages were exceptionally low. Five additional trades thus acquired Trade Boards before the Act of 1919 brought in the further criterion for setting up Trade Boards that "no adequate machinery exists for the effective regulation of wages throughout the trade". This criterion was retained in the 1945 Wages Councils Act.

The condition which State intervention aims to counteract is thus not clear cut. "Unduly" low implied that there is a "duly" low wage which did not qualify a trade for Trade Boards and exceptionally low implies a comparison with some "ruling" rate of wages which may not in fact prevail. This lack of clarity, criticized by the Cave Committee appointed in 1921 to review the work of the Boards, was according to Sir Henry Clay, wise.

"To complain that the Acts give no guidance, in the form of some principle by which the minimum wage should be fixed, was to overlook the practical wisdom that inspired them. What principle could have been laid down? The Cave Committee itself in spite of its complaints while recommending that the Boards be restricted to fixing minima, gave no guidance as to the principles on which such minima should be fixed."[1]

Criticism of lack of clarity of principles and also of definition of trades, and criticism of delay in adjusting rates to economic circumstances would, Clay considers, all be allayed if it were

[1] *The Problem of Industrial Relations*, 1929, p. 233.

realized that the Trade Boards were essentially organs of collective bargaining. The difficulty of definition derives from the nature of the industry itself, in which there are no sharp lines of demarcation into non-competing groups, and has nothing to do with Trade Boards as such. Delays in adjusting rates to changed conditions are no greater in Trade Board industries than in others.

We may well be reminded of the complexities and lags of industry and of the slight direct force which British public opinion desires the State to exert, so long as the aim can be achieved by *laissez-faire*. Clay's view that the State wage-fixing structures are "essentially organs of collective bargaining" has, as we shall see, received wide support, and was indeed acknowledged in the Wages Councils Act of 1945 when "no adequate" wage-regulating "machinery" was virtually made the sole test of an industry's need for a Council. Nevertheless the presence of a chairman and independent members appointed by the State before whom the two contending parties may feel called upon to parade objective grounds of appeal, may have made, and may still make some difference. At least two grounds appear upon which such an appeal can be based: that of correcting a wage unduly low when compared with the cost of living and its changes; and that of correcting a wage exceptionally low when compared with wages in similar work. The first correction implies the aim of a "living" wage, the second the aim of a "fair" wage. How far can these aims be expressed as measurable targets which the State could objectively use as criteria?

Several of the earlier Trade Boards, according to the Cave Committee "had regard only to the cost of living". The Committee in their report recommend that the Boards should aim "at giving protection to the workers in each trade by securing to them at least a wage which approximates to the subsistence level in the place in which they live", and (here in Pigou's words, "shirking" and leaving "an unmeaning chaos"[1]) "which the trade can bear".

Food is the chief element in subsistence and in recent years research into the physiology and biochemistry of diet has made sufficient progress to lay down the minimum food requirements in

[1] *Essays in Applied Economics*, 1923, p. 68.

terms of calories, mainly for energy, and vitamins, mainly for health and avoiding disease. Before such requirements can be translated into a sum of money, articles of food must be analysed for their calory and vitamin and also mineral content and those articles priced and repriced from time to time. Complicated as this process may appear, involving various sampling and index-number techniques, it is scientifically possible. One man's earnings may be required to keep alive a large family, another man's only himself, and a "standard" family had in fact to be formulated—usually man, wife and three children. (This *standard*, is by no means the same as the *average* family size which is smaller, since it is only a minority even among adult men, who have three or more children at home and dependent on their earnings. The majority is composed of single men, of newly-weds, and of the middle-aged and elderly whose children are earning for themselves or have left the home.) Where the number of dependent children requires a "living" wage higher than the standard, the gap has, since 1945, been at least to some degree bridged by family allowances and a standard living wage, brought up to date through index numbers of changes in the cost of living, thus provides a fairly realistic and measurable target. With rising prosperity there is now less emphasis on bare cost of living and more on a "human needs" standard including (as the index does) certain "conventional" necessaries like beer and tobacco.

A "fair" wage, on the other hand, involves fundamental difficulties of measurement. Allowance being made for differences in the steadiness of the demand for labour in different industries, wages are fair, writes Pigou[1] when "they are about on a level with the payment for tasks in other trades which are of equal difficulty and disagreeableness and which require equally rare natural abilities and an equally expensive training". The cost of training, including missed opportunities of earning, can perhaps be measured; but how can difficulty, disagreeableness and rarity of abilities? Job-evaluation has, it is true, made some progress within narrow ranges of occupation, but as economists may well point out, it is entirely concerned with the supply side. Jobs like the puddling of pig-iron or making chains by hand are difficult

[1] *Economics of Welfare*, 1920, p. 505.

and (to most people) disagreeable, and would get a high job rating, yet they are becoming valueless because no longer demanded. Rarity can it is true be measured (the number of persons with six toes could no doubt be sampled) but it is not rarity in itself that is "fairly" paid high, but tasks in high demand that require rare ability—quite another matter.

In the practice of wage-bargaining, "fair" has come to mean "customary", "traditional", "related to established status". A policy of fair wages thus means a conservative policy of maintaining the *status quo*, maintaining the old "relativities" and wage-differentials between grades and occupations, between ages and sexes. The aim of this policy is not one of defending one party in industry against another in spite of economic and social forces, but rather of participating with those forces for the smooth and unhindered running of the mechanism. The State-established and partially State-nominated Wages Councils with their encouragement of appeals to a living wage and a fair wage may have deflected the policy of "*laissez collectives faire*" however slightly towards the aims of avoiding starvation wages at the bottom of the scale but conservatively maintaining "fair" differentials higher up the scale, as far as the two are compatible.

In times of full employment a third aim might, however, be expected from the Wages Councils, that of "manning up" industries of high national importance by offering them higher wages than industries of less importance. This policy would, by popular judgment, count as eminently "unfair" to incumbents of the less important industries. Though it is the hub of a national wages policy, and in spite of shortages of man-power in coal, in export trades and basic manufacture, this aim has in fact not been attempted through the mechanism of Wages Councils, or even, as described later, of arbitration, even though the State takes such a large part in wage fixing. Traditional belief in *laissez-faire* as expressed particularly strongly in substance (though not words) by the Trade Unions, has here in fact, proved too strong. The possible future of such a State wage policy will be discussed later. It is not a policy of defence of one party from the action of another, but one of control over the whole industrial economy.

§4 *Success and Future of the Wages Councils*

Success is measured by the degree to which aims are achieved, and to measure the success of any State policy defending one party from another, the precise aims of the defence must be kept in mind. No very precise guidance about aims was given officially in the original Trade Boards Act, or in subsequent orders, but the first interpretation of aims by the Boards was avoidance of sweating and poverty by a legally enforced minimum wage, in all industries where "unduly" or "exceptionally" low wages prevailed. This aim appears to have been achieved. The Cave Committee found that "speaking generally, Trade Boards have succeeded in abolishing the grosser forces of under-payment and regularizing wages conditions. . . . (They) have afforded protection to the good employer, able and willing to pay a reasonable rate of remuneration to his workers, from unscrupulous competitors, prepared to take unfair advantage of the economic necessities of their workers".[1]

The gloomy prognosticators about "interference" by the State had not however denied that wages could be raised. They were chiefly worried about the repercussions of "artificial" wage-rates upon employment. A Trade Board might coerce employers into raising wages but it could not at the same time coerce them into keeping the same numbers employed and the prognostication was that the demand curve for labour being "elastic", the higher the price of labour the less labour would be demanded—the undemanded becoming unemployed.

This expectation made at least one or other of three assumptions unwarranted by the facts of the real industrial situation.

(*a*) It assumed that under competition the bulk of (surviving) employers were fairly equally efficient.

(*b*) It ignored the effect of the "jolt" of higher wages on the use of more efficient and less costly methods of production.

(*c*) It assumed that though different units of labour were admittedly not equally willing or capable at any one time, changes in willingness and capacity would not be effected. In short, it assumed a constant distribution of capacities, morale and unrest. Today we are accustomed to the notion of varying labour productivity, varying both from firm to firm and from

[1]Cmd. 1645, 1922, p. 23.

time to time, which can be stimulated to vary upwards, for instance, by reduction of fatigue or by incentives.

Productivity per worker may as a result of fixing a minimum wage increase, in any one industry, by six routes.

(i) The physiological route through increased working capacity. Some wages below the minimum may have provided the workers with too little food, when shared with his dependents, for the energy required in the work to be done, particularly if the working hours were long. With a higher wage the worker may be enabled to work faster and to lose less time by sickness and fatigue. A "virtuous circle" is established whereby higher wages result in greater capacity to earn higher wages.

(ii) The psychological route of giving workers a definite standard of living for which they will strive. With a higher wage at the bottom of the scale, some, though not all, workers (depending on their level of aspiration) will cease to have a casual happy-go-lucky attitude and will work to a target.

(iii) The inter-industry transfer route. The higher pay may attract more capable and willing workers into the industry from other industries, or keep them when they would otherwise leave. Increased productivity that will "pay" the higher wages is obtained by acquiring and keeping a more productive type of worker within the industry.

(iv) The inter-firm transfer route, indicated by the quotation from the Cave Committee. The "good" employer already paying the minimum wage, might indeed be more than "protected" from his "unscrupulous" wage-cutting competitors. If the unscrupulous were also inefficient and went out of business because productivity per worker in his employ was too low to enable the minimum wages to be paid, then his trade might well be transferred to the good employers and his workers find employment with them.

(v) The reorganizational route, pointed out by J. W. F. Rowe.[1] Higher wages stimulate employers to change the form of their organization so as to reduce costs, including the introduction of machinery or of more efficient machinery. In the short run, this may diminish employment but in the long run (granting some competition and an elastic demand for the product) prices are likely to fall and sales to increase.

[1] *Wages in Theory and Practice*, 1928.

C

(vi) The transfer plus reorganization route. It is not necessary for every firm to reorganize. If only some reorganize so as to increase productivity and reduce costs and prices, they will compete successfully against firms who did not reorganize and, with increased sales, they will be able to take on the workers originally employed by the unregenerate firms.

Tailoring was the largest industry covered by any one of the original Trade Boards of 1909, and results in 1913–14 were reviewed by Tawney. He was under the necessity of pointing out that economists' assumptions were unreal.

"If it is not explicitly stated, it is constantly assumed, that at any one moment an industry is organized in the most efficient way which the resources of science make possible, and that the "representative firm" is one which is perpetually endeavouring to introduce the latest improvements in organization, machinery and general equipment. . . . In reality, except in a few strongly organized industries, no assumption could be further from the truth. What is true is that competition does keep competing employers up to the mark *in those matters which come within their immediate purview*, and the significance of which needs no special effort either for their understanding or for their application. No man buys dear if he can buy cheap, or sells cheap if he can sell dear. But there are a large number of matters which do not ordinarily come within the purview of more than a small number of exceptionally enlightened employers, because they have not any immediate competitive significance, and, with regard to these, the actual practice of employers is no guide to the practice which is either economically or socially most beneficial."[1]

Tawney proceeds to quote Mr. Seebohm Rowntree "himself a large employer" in his support:

"It may be argued that employers only pay low wages because it is to their advantage to do so; that they are so shrewd, and competition is so keen, that if efficiency wages were more profitable, they would always be paid. However valid such an argument appears, like many theoretical arguments it will be found to have very little validity if tested by actual experience. . . . Employers, like other people, get into ruts, and the payment of low wages may be the result, not of a carefully thought-out policy, but of an old custom which might very profitably be superseded."

[1] *Minimum Rates in the Tailoring Industry*, 1915, pp. 157–8.

In his earlier study of Trade Boards in the chain-making industry, Tawney thought that "the ingenuity of employers and workpeople so greatly exceeds that of economists that discussions of what "must" happen, unsupported by evidence of what has happened, or is happening, are usually quite worthless".[1] The collection of "evidence of what has happened or is happening" started a hundred years ago by Lord Brassey has been continued by J. A. Hobson, R. H. Tawney himself, and J. W. F. Rowe, and now by a host of industrial psychologists and sociologists, industrial economists and, like Seebohm Rowntree, economist industrialists. The upshot is that far greater weight is now given to the expansive possibilities of management and workers in response to a higher wage.

The belief in the Economy of High Wages enunciated by Brassey and Hobson,[2] and the realization that high wages did not necessarily mean high labour costs has now become a belief in the almost unlimited wage possibilities of high productivity. The possibility however can only become probability if managers are properly selected and trained and workers cast off their assumption of a fixed work fund and their insistence upon traditional working methods. In most cases it is not so much harder work that is required as willing adaptation to new techniques—to new work-methods and to multiple shifts, for instance. Above all both parties must *want* to produce more— a consummation that by no means holds universally today. If employers, managers and workers prefer an easy life to aspiring towards a higher standard of living and working, then they must be content with lower profits, lower salaries and lower wages. It is up to them to choose. But the fact remains that the resources of modern industry *can* meet the higher wages fixed by the Wages Councils, and can do so without loss of employment.

Wages Councils are not however likely greatly to be extended in the future. Wages so low that the result necessarily was primary poverty and semi-starvation have by now been abolished. The avowed primary aim of Wages Boards is no longer to avoid wages unduly low, but exclusively to supplement voluntary collective bargaining.

[1] *Establishment of Minimum Rates in the Chain-making Industry*, 1914, p. 105.
[2] *Evolution of Capitalism*, 1917, Chapter XIV.

Reviewing the wage decisions of the Councils over a number of years up to 1954 Barbara Wootton is forced[1] to the conclusions of Clay in 1923, already given (p. 60) and of many a skilled mediator like C. W. Guillebaud[2]

"The ostensible object is to make good any gaps left in the voluntary arrangements for collective bargaining. Logically, such a transformation of Wages Councils into a kind of statutory substitute for spontaneous collective bargaining would seem to imply that the Councils should behave as nearly as possible as, in similar circumstances, voluntary negotiating bodies would have behaved; that they should envisage their role as that of bargaining instruments, rather than as the means of putting into effect high principles of social policy."

The State, in short, appears so keen on the *laissez collectives faire* policy, that in industries where voluntary collectives fail to appear, the State is apt to create relations artificially by means of equivalent structures participating in the collective bargaining. Except that the voluntary collective structures were missing on the labour rather than the employers' side, the recent policy exercised through the Wages Councils cannot be said to have been defence of one party from another for the sake of greater equality or stability or any other national aim; but rather the smooth running of the industrial machine, and the conservation of existing social relations.

With the growth of Trade Unions into an "Estate of the Realm" (as Sir Winston Churchill has put it), and their recognition—and, indeed, imitation—by Employers' Associations, the gap left over from State-less "voluntary" collective bargaining is narrowing. There is, in short, no more room for proliferating Wages Councils in further industries, and some industries, for instance, furniture and tobacco, have already abandoned the Wages Council procedure in favour of procedures with less State interference. The real wages of workers will be defended or increased in most industries mainly by the collective bargaining between workers and employers in which the State only occasionally participates—a participation that Chapter IV will describe and discuss.

[1] *The Social Foundations of Wage Policy*, 1955, pp. 85–6.
[2] Ministry of Labour, *The Worker in Industry*, 1951, pp. 43–54.

§5 *The Defence of the Shareholder*

Industrialization has resulted in industrial workers without capital of their own in their industry. It has also resulted in a large number of industrial capitalists without work in their industry. Control has been divorced not only from the workers in the firm but from the owners of the firm's capital. Though by the paper constitution of the Joint Stock Companies the shareholders have the legal rights of ultimate control, in actual operation power has accrued to the profit-taking financiers, the salaried managers and fee'd directors. J. A. Hobson has referred[1] to "a great capitalist proletariat, who bear to the operators of finance a relation closely analogous to that which the labouring proletariat bear to the employing class. The ordinary investor, the small capitalist, must sell the use of his capital, as the labourer must sell the use of his labours, to some organizer of a business enterprise if he is to get any advantage from possessing it." The worker has required State protection from the management through Factory Acts and Wages Councils; the Joint Stock shareholder has received similar protection by the State, mainly through the Company Acts.

What are the hazards to the shareholder that would justify deviation from *laissez-faire*? The role of keeping the ring, which *laissez-faire* allows the State, involved some form of Company Law to regulate the behaviour of the company towards the people it traded with and in particular its obligations as debtor. At first, shareholders were obliged to meet the claims of their company's creditors to the full extent of all their private property. But in a series culminating in 1855–56, the Limited Liability Acts protected the shareholders in certain companies and limited his liability to the extent of his share. Gradually, the Company Acts advanced from the role of keeping the ring between independent traders and guarding mainly against fraud, towards the role of defending, like the Factory Acts, one party within an industrial organization from another.

The Joint Stock Company is the creation of the State, the creature of statutes, and it is logical enough for the State to interfere between the parties it has created. But further to justify this deviation from *laissez-faire* three propositions may be proved.

[1]*Evolution of Capitalism*, 1917, pp. 241–2.

(i) That the shareholder is useful and important, and that there is no other equally efficient alternative source of risk capital. In short, that the private shareholder is necessary to the economy.

(ii) That he cannot look after his own interests.

(iii) That he is likely to be exploited.

The situation is similar to that of the worker, except that the necessity of the worker is taken for granted, and there is no need to prove his usefulness and importance.

(i) Risk, or to be more specific (since they are not calculable actuarially), "uncertainties", arise inevitably from the technical and market circumstances of whole industries and from the management and policy of the separate firms within the industry. In the Joint Stock Company the ordinary shareholder paid by dividend out of the profit, much of which is ploughed back, bears these unavoidable risks.

The main alternative source of risk-capital to that of shares is the ploughing back of company reserves into its own business. This method holds the disadvantage that the new capital usually goes back into the old bottles and unless the company integrates a wide mixture of industries the direction of new capital is restricted and the economy likely to be ossified. New shares can, on the contrary, be issued by firms in any industry, though for effective mobility and direction of capital knowledgeable and intelligent potential shareholders are needed, able to judge what industries and companies are likely to be successful.

(ii) Like labour, the shareholder can (at least in public companies) leave the organization and, if he wishes, join another, thus suiting his own interest. He can sell his holding on the Stock Exchange. The catch, however, is that if too many investors (or a few large holders) in the company take the same view of their interests, the price of the shares will, with this high shareholder "turnover", fall considerably.

Unlike labour, however, the shareholder has the legal right of controlling his firm. The Joint Stock Company is a structure created—or, to be exact, "incorporated"—by the State, and the Golden Rule (to quote Sir Dennis Robertson), is that control goes with risk. The ordinary shareholder is given a vote on the appointment of directors, the declaration of dividend and other policies brought before the shareholders' meeting, and is usually entitled to a vote in exact proportion to his holding of shares. But in real fact, though *not* in law, unless he, or he and his friends, own a majority or a large minority of the shares, the shareholder is usually powerless. As I sum up elsewhere:

"Normally, shareholders' meetings (ordinary or extraordinary) only exercise real control when transactions have gone wrong and dividends cannot be paid—but usually so wrong that the company or corporation faces bankruptcy and control is in fact and in law rapidly slipping from shareholders to debenture or bond holders, or a bank or other creditors."[1]

Moreover it is possible under Company Law to issue classes of ordinary shares without votes, and to give certain classes more votes than others. A holder, or a "holding company" owning a few high-voting shares may thus control policy, however conscientiously the holders of the majority of lower-voting shares attend meetings or send proxies. The risk-taking control of policy is thus, in practice, usually divorced from risk-bearing.

(iii) Is the ordinary risk-bearing shareholder in fact likely to be exploited as a result of his lack of control over company policy? Exploitation in his case refers either to avoidable loss or to insufficient compensation for bearing the *un*avoidable risk, or uncertainty.

What is a sufficient compensation must depend on the psychological aversion of potential investors to bearing the sort of risks presented by industry. In spite of the widespread betting propensities among the community, it appears that security and the absence of risk, is as highly valued by the industrial investor as by the industrial worker and therefore that deviations from full security must be highly compensated. Apart from changes in prices and the value of money, full security may be represented by the post-office savings bank, where $2\frac{1}{2}$ per cent is paid per annum, and the exact money capital put in can be quickly got out. On the other hand the capital invested in ordinary industrial shares (less cost of stamp duty and commission) may be paid a fluctuating dividend, and, with a fall in stock exchange values, may not be got out in full, if at all.

[1]Florence, *Logic of British and American Industry*, 1953, p. 186.

There is usually a wide variation from year to year in the general level of profits of companies as a whole; and £100 invested in any one year may in the course of years, show a wide variation in gain according to the particular company in which it was invested. In the fifteen years 1936–51, about a sixth of all industrial and commercial and brewery companies with over a million issued capital showed a gain to the investor by dividend, bonus shares and capital appreciation of less than the 37½ per cent obtainable in post-office savings; and among the smaller companies comparative losses seem to have been greater, quite apart from some complete failures.[1] At the top end of the scale the gain was not the immediate thousandfold prize of a lottery but a mere six or sevenfold gain over the fifteen years. Human nature seems averse to this shape of risk, though the middle range and average results were far more favourable than in betting. Betting occurs on risks that can be actuarially calculated and odds given, and where the "shape" and timing of the risk is different to that of industrial investment. Betting offers a slight chance of a great immediate gain rather than industry's large chance of a small gain, some time ahead—a shape that appears unpopular.

It is possible therefore to hold that over a fairly long period, and taking one company with another, shareholders in industry are liable to exploitation to the extent of insufficient payment for the unpopular risks and uncertainties borne. This insufficiency of compensation acts as a deterrent; if more (and more intelligent) risk and uncertainty bearing is required in the national interest, the State must try to remove the causes of high risk and uncertainty, as well as the deterrents to hearing whatever part of risk and uncertainty is unavoidable.

The main cause is the ignorance of the investor, or potential investor. Coming events in the economic world are uncertain enough, even if present and past events are known; if they are not known it is likely either that the potential investor will not risk investment or that he will invest, but lose more than if he were not ignorant. To stimulate intelligent investment, therefore,

---

[1]Based on research by G. M. Lawrence and P. Sargant Florence, University of Birmingham, under the Conditional Aid scheme for the use of Counterpart Funds, derived from U.S. Economic Aid.

the State has for a long time compelled disclosure of facts by Public Joint Stock Companies through various devices: publication of the names of directors; a register of shareholders open to public inspection; annual presentation of balance sheet and profit and loss or income and expenditure account; an independent auditor appointed by shareholders; finally, inspection by the Board of Trade if requested by a number of shareholders owning a sufficient proportion of shares.

Where the relatively low compensation for risk-bearing is due to a low total of dividends this is the *immediate* outcome of the directors' policy in the allocation of profits. The proportion of earnings declared as dividend can normally only be revised downward by the shareholders' meeting; for reasons already given, if not obvious, revision is seldom suggest. Low total earnings in relation to the need for reinvestment is, however, the ultimate cause of low dividends and earnings are partly the outcome of directors' policy, partly of unavoidable events.

If the first practical line of defence of shareholders is more information in general, their second line consists in specific defences from action adverse to their interests (*a*) by directors, (*b*) by fellow shareholders and (*c*) by promoters.

(*a*) Three types of defence from directors are written by the State into company law:

(i) greater power by shareholders over directors;
(ii) participation of directors in shareholding and public knowledge of their share transactions; and
(iii) public knowledge of their remuneration.

(i) The Board of Directors are often inclined to identify the company with themselves and, for instance, to accuse shareholders of a want of loyalty if they are tempted by high take-over bids to sell their shares to business interests seeking to displace the directors. But it is the shareholders who are legally the proprietors, and new legislation tries to make the legal proprietors more effective in determining policy. The Companies Act of 1948 largely followed the recommendations of the Cohen Committee for increasing the power of shareholders over directors, or at least diminishing their powerlessness.

Previous to the Act shareholders' meetings might be called

c*

by the Board of Directors at very short notice and the whole
machinery by which the shareholders were approached was in
the hands of the Board, shareholders being invited, for instance,
to appoint directors as their proxies. Under the Act of 1948
at least three weeks' notice must be given of the annual meeting
and two weeks of other meetings. Proceedings of the Board
must be entered in books open to shareholders' inspection, and
full information not only of the Board's but (if sufficiently
backed) of opposition resolutions, and of all matters to be
dealt with at shareholders' meetings, must be circulated. The
proxy forms sent to shareholders must make it clear that they
can appoint persons who are not shareholders and that they
can vote for or against the Board's resolutions.

Strengthening shareholders by allowing for more effective
discussion of policy can be supported by greater powers in
appointing and dismissing directors, or, at least, less inertia.
Though by law the electors of the directorate, "in fact the shareholders neither initiate nor discuss, but merely confirm as though
by rubber stamp, the election of the directors. Evidence has
accumulated that directors to be elected or re-elected are
nominated by the existing directors, or a group of them; and
normally there is only one list of nominees. The system of
election is, in short, co-option and single-party co-option at
that".[1]

Co-opting directors may well, as the Cohen Committee
put it, "feel it difficult to raise the question" of an age limit for
their colleagues, and Miller and Campbell found in 1933[2] among
a large sample of directors the remarkable proportion of 57 per
cent over sixty (the age when civil servants retire) and 42 per
cent over sixty-five (the age when University professors retire).
To give more frequent change in appointment whether by
genuine election or co-option the Act of 1948 lays down (para.
185) that "no person shall be capable of being appointed a
director of a company . . . if at the time of his appointment he
has attained the age of seventy". This limit laid down by the
State is subject, however, to many provisos, and special
procedures may be adopted by companies to circumvent its
application.

[1]Florence, *op. cit.* p. 177.   [2]*Financial Democracy*, p. 98.

(ii) The articles of most companies require that directors must each have a certain qualifying minimum of shares, presumably to give them an identity of interest with all shareholders. In fact, a large proportion of directors do not hold more than the minimum and these minima are a very small proportion indeed of the total capital. Directors' holdings range very widely in different companies but it is worth bearing in mind that the average director of all large British industrial and commercial companies (with over three million capital) held in 1935, under his own name only ¼ per cent of the nominal value of shares.[1]

(iii) In addition to the disclosure of all the holdings of directors and of their share transactions, a specific safeguard may be the compulsory disclosure of directors' remuneration. The former disclosure helps to defend, or at least to warn, the shareholders against directors' possible failure to identify the interests of the proprietors with their own; the latter to warn the shareholder against a particular failure of identification by directors, that of "lining their own pockets" at the expense of the company. The Companies Act of 1948, following the Cohen Committee's proposal, lays down (section 196 (1)) that in any accounts of a company there shall be shown the aggregate amount of the directors' emoluments and that distinction should be made between emoluments as a director and otherwise, for instance as a full-time manager.

(b) State defence of the shareholder or potential shareholder is not confined, however, to defence against the directors of the company in which he holds or may hold shares. By experience it has been found that he may have to be defended from at least two other possible foci of exploitation: from fellow-shareholders, especially directors of holding companies that own a predominant holding in his company, and from promoters trying to float a company.

The holding company owning 50 per cent or more but not 100 per cent of the shares of the subsidiary company is technically just a fellow shareholder of the other shareholders of the subsidiary—just a "big brother". But its policy, which can dominate that of the subsidiary, is not under the control of these other shareholders. Thus determination of the policy is

[1] *op. cit.* p. 209.

once removed from the subsidiary's other shareholders; and if the holding company is itself a subsidiary of a super-holding company—a not infrequent occurrence—determination is twice removed. There may be even longer chains of subsidiaries and sub-subsidiaries with further removal of control and a holding of less than 50 per cent may frequently give virtual control. Thus power may be concentrated in quite a small fraction of shareholders at the apex of the pyramid of control. Certainly control under these circumstances is far removed from the risk-bearing "little brother" shareholders. The State can perhaps not do much more for them than to get the facts disclosed about the extent of the controlling holding(s) and (particularly if the holder is a private company or trust not liable to disclose essential information) about the nature of the holders. The manipulation of accounts between subsidiary companies and companies holding 50 per cent or more of its voting shares is now countered by the Companies Act's insistence upon consolidated accounts for the whole group of holding and subsidiary companies. But the difference in power between 50 per cent and 40 per cent or even a 30 per cent holding is often only legalistic. The State may well, therefore (as the Cohen Committee recommended in vain), compel the register of shareholders to name the real beneficiary (and not, as now allowed, just his nominee) of all holdings exceeding a certain proportion of the whole issue. The U.S. Securities and Exchange Commission Act introduced this rule for all holdings exceeding a proportion as low as 2 per cent.

(c) To the promoter and the "prospectus" which he presents to prospective shareholders the State pays more attention than to possible exploitation by fellow shareholders. The risks of shareholders are indeed greatest in the early life of a company. The Companies Act lays down what facts are to be stated in the prospectus and persons contravening this regulation are liable to a heavy fine. But the State also relies on a certain participation by responsible private institutions, such as the Press and the Stock Exchange. So that the Press can have full scope to comment and possibly to expose misleading prospectuses, the Cohen Committee recommended a compulsory interval of at least two days between the publication of the prospectus and the opening of the lists to subscribers for shares, and suggested that fears of proceedings for libel should be allayed. "Some of the requirements of the London Stock Exchange Committee as to the information to be disclosed in prospectuses and advertisements go beyond the requirements of the Companies Act. . . . If the . . . committee is not satisfied, they can refuse permission to deal."[1]

To sum up, the practical aim of State action in defence of the shareholder is primarily economic, to allow incentives to work freely, or at least to check deterrents, so that the necessary supply of risk capital will be forthcoming. A philosophical aim may also be present of a more equal diffusion of ownership. This aim was avowed in the report of the Liberal Industrial Inquiry. In a chapter headed the *Diffusion of Ownership*, a subsection discussed the "Difficulties of the Small Investor", and the following section "Means of Encouraging Industrial Investment". The difficulties included banks' discouragement of small accounts; the mysteriousness of the machinery of investment; obstacles to purchasing shares by instalment; and, finally, the inability to get good advice and to distribute shares wisely, when there is only a small capital to invest.

Though historically the sponsor of *laissez-faire*, the Liberal Party, as represented by the influential inquiry committee, including Lord Keynes, did not hesitate to conclude that "a very great expansion of popular saving and investment is necessary in the national interest"; that the developments required for the purpose "need to be supervised and regulated for the protection of the investor; and that this duty should be imposed upon the Board of Trade or (a) proposed Ministry of Industry".[2]

§6 *The Defence of the Independent Trader, and the Consumer*

The discussion of the State's activity in defending third parties has referred up to the present to the defence of one party from another within any industrial organization, particularly labour and the shareholder. Now we pass to the State's defence of independent persons or independent organizations in industry, one from another. Exploitation is usually thought of

[1]Cmd. 6659, 1945, par. 24.
[2]*Britain's Industrial Future*, 1928, Chapter XIX.

as selling goods to the consumer at a price unduly high because it incorporates an unnecessarily high profit or is based on relatively inefficient production. But the notion may be extended on the one hand to anyone selling the consumer harmful or poor quality goods and, on the other, to the industrialist possessing some degree of monopoly and the power to sell at an unduly high price to other traders; or possessing some degree of monopsony and the power to buy at an unduly low price from suppliers and from the independent inventor.

Laissez-faire about the quality of goods sold to the consumer is based on the supposition that the buyer knows what he wants and can be left to judge by inspection or experience. *Caveat emptor*, let the buyer beware! But, by the same token as Mill's exception that "the uncultivated cannot be competent judges of cultivation", the unscientific cannot be competent judges of science. "A man," Jevons supposes, "about to buy a mansion tries the water out of the well, and is satisfied by its sparkling limpidity and its brisk taste. A chemist would have pointed out that these are suspicious symptoms and analysis might have detected deadly sewage poison".[1] The State now compels the information disclosed by scientific analysis to be displayed on the labels of bottles of mineral waters and patent medicines. But progress in the science of food values and medicinal drugs may well justify further State defence of the consumer (beyond mere information) from harmful industrial products or even harmless products that pretend to values or strengths they do not possess. And the defence will adopt Factory-Act, rather than more participatory procedures. Just as direct rule by the State is important to defend the worker from factory conditions, the precise danger of which to life, health and limb he cannot judge, so a consumer should be defended in his own interests from eating substances of which he cannot measure the unwholesomeness or the lack of nutritional or medicinal value. The State thus lays down standards of purity in food or drugs which it will directly enforce, for instance, a specific proportion of artificial preservative in jam which is not to be exceeded.

Food, Drug or Adulteration Acts, or sections of Public
___
[1] *The State in Relation to Labour* (1882), Ed. 1910, p. 43.

Health Acts such as were passed in 1872 and 1875 deviate from *laissez-faire*, and can be vindicated by the superior knowledge of specialists advising or employed by the State over the ordinary consumer. The Ministry of Food now contains departments for research and the discovery of new knowledge with a scientific advisers' division, linking it to scientific and medical committees and food research organizations. The Ministry also contains departments for spreading that knowledge (e.g. the Information Branch); and departments for drafting new laws and orders based on that knowledge, and for inspection and the enforcement of these laws and orders, often in conjunction with local authorities.

The manufacturing of food products employs more workers in Britain today than agriculture and fishing put together, so that the defence of the consumer from poor quality food is largely a relation of the State to industry. More purely industrial in its activity is the maintenance of standards of quality and performance in durable manufactured goods either for the industrial user or the final consumer. The State may either brand products itself or support their branding by industry. Which of the two policies is adopted largely depends, as Jevons pointed out[1], on the "simplicity" of the product.

"No ordinary person can possibly judge the quality of a watch which, from all that appears to the unpractised eye, might be worth £10 or £50. Nevertheless, it is out of the question that Government officers should be employed to inspect and stamp watches before they are allowed to be exposed for sale. The sufficient reason is, no doubt, that watches differ infinitely in details of construction and finish, so that it would be impossible to say exactly what the certification meant, or how long it would hold good. The fineness of the gold or silver composing the case is a simple definite fact which can be tested in a few moments and exactly recorded. . . . We may perhaps infer that Government branding is only to be approved under the following joint conditions—(1) When some special danger is to be avoided, or some special considerable advantage to be attained by Government intervention; (2) When the individual is not able to exercise proper judgment and supervision on his own behalf; (3) When the intervention required is of a simple and certain character, and the results can be certified in a manner comprehensible to all."

[1] *op. cit.* p. 50.

For the more complicated industrial products, State policy must be indirect devolution: by Trade or Merchandise Marks Acts (e.g. 1862, 1887 and 1953), to register and protect the brands and marks of individual or associations of private firms against imitation and lowering of quality; and by subsidy or exclusive privileges to encourage a certain grading or hall-marking through institutions which industry itself has set up such as Stationers' Hall and the British Standards Institution. To economize cloth during the last war manufacturers agreed with the government to bulk-produce marked "utility" clothing of adequate but economic material to a standard design at a given low price. Recently the British Standards Institution, which began with engineering specifications, has formed a Women's Advisory Committee, which represents over a score of national organizations, and issues a quarterly *Consumer Report*.

Advocates have, however, appeared for more direct and positive State action in setting up consumer research to test the qualities claimed by branded and advertised products and to praise and blame accordingly. British libel laws are held to frighten private organizations such as exist in America; so (short of altering these laws) the State, it is held, must step in where the individual fears to tread, and should analyse durable products (as the State and local authorities already analyse suspected food, without, however, disclosing the maker), and should inform the public of the result of its analysis.

Within the last few years, however, the quality of products offered the consumer has been overtaken in the attention of the State by the more quantitative, economic, problems of monopoly.

The policy of *laissez-faire* on monopoly exploitation, recognized by an Act of 1844 abolishing the offences of engrossing, forestalling and regrating, had continued in Britain until as recently as 1948. This continuance was partly due to the strength of the theory deprecating State interference, as against the weakness of the organization of consumers; partly to the relative absence, or supposed absence, till recently, of monopoly in Britain. Up to the start of the First World War it was maintained by economists, both at home and abroad, that Britain was peculiarly free of monopoly compared with other large industrial countries like Germany and, above all, the United

States of America. Though in America the federal government had taken action against monopoly as early as 1890 with the passage of the Sherman Anti-Trust Act, and later, in 1914, the Clayton Act, the matter was left in Britain to the Common Law of restraint of trade. And on the whole, Common Law came in this period to take a lenient view and to allow "reasonable" restraint. Meanwhile, however, British firms were growing larger, tariffs were introduced in 1932, and by 1931–35 it was doubtful whether the concentration of single industries in a few hands was not the same, approximately, in Britain as in America.[1] Moreover, trade associations between firms became very noticeable in certain industries. During the First World War, the Government made use of the associations in order to co-ordinate the war effort of single firms, but became sufficiently alarmed at their probable extension, for the Ministry of Reconstruction to appoint a committee on Trusts, which reported in 1918. No State action followed this service of information and publicity. Indeed, in the inter-war period, State action as well as inaction appeared, whatever the complexion of the government, to favour monopoly, as giving some security against the industrial depression. The Coal Mines Act of 1930 set up under the control of the industry, a system of central and district output quotas with fines if they were exceeded, largely to keep up the price of coal, raise the profit of owners and, while reducing their hours, raise the wages of miners. A committee on Restraint of Trade reported in 1931 against interference with resale price maintenance.

During the Second as during the First World War much use was made, for the sake of co-ordination, of trade associations, and their power had greatly increased by the close of the war. Several *ad hoc* committees were appointed to investigate these trade associations and practices—notably the fforde Committee on Cement Costs, reporting in 1946, the Simon Committee on the Distribution of Building Materials and Components, reporting in 1948, and the Lloyd Jacob Committee on Resale Price Maintenance, reporting in 1949.

In 1948, by the Monopolies and Restrictive Practices Act, a permanent Monopolies and Restrictive Practices Commission

[1]Florence, *Logic of British and American Industry*, 1953, pp. 131–5.

was set up; in 1953, the maximum number of Commissioners was increased from ten to twenty-five. Based on complaints mostly from traders rather than consumers, the Commission has issued a number of reports on a selection of separate industries (most of them small) and separate products; and one report on the "general reference" of Collective Discrimination. These reports established the facts about monopolistic conditions and arrangements, and judged whether they were or were not against the public interest, making recommendations if necessary. Usually the Board of Trade to whom the Commission reported, induced the trade itself under threat of an order, to change practices and policies found to be against the public interest.

In 1956, a stronger State procedure attacking the problem as a whole and not piece-meal, industry by industry, was introduced under the Restrictive Trade Practices Act. A court, normally to sit in divisions, is set up of "five judges and up to ten lay persons having knowledge of or experience in industry, commerce or public affairs". Agreements must be registered and the onus of showing that they are in the public interest is now to rest with those who wish to continue restrictive practices; arguments however (including serious and persistent unemployment if they were removed) are laid down which a trade association can use to justify such practices. In any case, practices are illegal if they "have operated or are calculated to operate to an unreasonable extent to the detriment of persons not parties to the agreement". These persons may be consumers affected by prices kept high directly or through practices keeping up costs of supply, and maintaining vested interests and unnecessarily elaborate services; or affected by deprivation of possible improvements or of a choice of goods. These persons may also be engaged or seeking to engage in trade, but pushed or kept out by boycott, quota schemes, deferred rebates, et al. Keeping other traders out makes for an easier life for the existing traders and an easy life often forms as strong an incentive toward monopoly as high profits. The old 1948 Commission, renamed the Monopoly Commission and reduced to no more than ten members is left to investigate (when required by the Board of Trade) single-firm restrictive practices or monopolies, exclusively export agreements and matters not covered by the 1956 Act.

The State is thus to concentrate on defence from certain practices, particularly if carried out by groups of firms rather than defence from monopoly in itself. An agreement between several manufacturers to enforce price maintenance is illegal, but individual maintenance by one manufacturer is enforcible through the civil courts. Monopoly must indeed be recognized as often holding public advantages. We have noted the growth of large plants and firms in the course of the industrial revolution, due to certain economies. The largest scale on which any product can be made obviously occurs when there is only one producer; where the total market of an industry is small but the economies of scale great, a single monopoly may have very much lower costs than a number of producers each on a small scale. Intrinsic economies of monopoly also arise, notably in avoiding overlap in spatial distribution as for piped gas and water supply, or avoiding waste of man-power in house-to-house deliveries.

The deviation from *laissez-faire* marked by the legislation since 1948 is thus aimed at a limited objective, and before leaving the Monopoly Commission or the Court set up by the Act of 1956, their activities or proposed activities must be placed in perspective among the related aims, policies and devices employed by the State. The general picture of the defences against monopoly is given in Table 2. Some practices harmful to the public interest may be considered temporary, and self-rectifying through supply and demand in the market without any State action; or curable, under policy II in the table, by a genuine *laissez-faire* that would abolish tariffs and modify patent laws. The general tariff introduced in 1932, though modified by the General Agreement on Tariffs and Trade (G.A.T.T.), still protects many British industries from foreign competition. Patents cannot now be used wholly to deprive the consumer of possible improvements since the State insists on a patentee granting licenses on "reasonable" terms if he is not using the patent himself. The consumer's interest requires, however, new inventions and for this reason patent law will have to compromise on the question which has exercised utilitarian philosophers like Sidgwick, how "to give adequate encouragement to the inventor protected, while hampering other inventors as little as possible".[1]

[1] *Elements of Politics*, 1908, p. 342.

TABLE 2: ALTERNATIVE STATE PROCEDURES AND LEGIS-
LATION IN THE DEFENCE FROM MONOPOLY
EXPLOITATION

I   *No Active Policy. Existing Level of Laissez-faire*
     Reliance upon existence of "Countervailing Power" (*e.g.* one
     monopoly fighting another), substitutes, or competing
     methods (*e.g.* Road and Rail).

II   *Back to Real Laissez-faire*
     Repeal, or Reduction of Tariffs
     Modification of Patent Law
     Repeal of State-sponsored Quotas (*e.g.* 1930 Coal Mines Act).

III *Introduce or Encourage Competition*
     Preferential Trading by existing State agencies
     General Post Office orders for independent cable firms[1]
     No State trading with (monopolistic) London builders[1]
     Creation of new State agencies, wholesaling, importing,
     purchasing
     State operation of competing organization
     State holding of shares in Joint Stock Companies
     Encouraging Consumers' Cooperative Societies

IV   *Discourage Practices Excluding or Hampering Possible Competition*
     Ending division of market, collusive bids, collective price
     maintenance, stop lists, quotas, allocations, etc., and their
     sanctions and organization of sanctions (*e.g.* boycotts,
     loyalty rebates, pooled profits and losses, private courts)
     (*a*) By assurances from the industry;
     (*b*) By Orders or Statutes, enforceable in Special, in Civil
     or in Criminal Courts.

V   *Direct Review and Regulation of Prices and Terms*
     Equality of treatment (allowing for lower costs of large orders)
     Gas Companies Acts: 1847, maximum prices; 1875, sliding
     scales of dividend against price
     Review of Associations' minimum prices so as, *e.g.* to give
     no more than a reasonable profit to the lowest-cost producer
     of each type of cable

VI   *Restructuring*
     Dissolution of Cartels and Trade Associations
     Break-up of Combines (*e.g.* Holding Companies)
     State operation of Monopoly

[1]*See* Monopoly Commission Reports on *Insulated Wires and Cables*, and
on the *Supply of Buildings in the Greater London Area.*

Policy III would allow the State positively to introduce or encourage competition. Proposals of this sort were made by the Monopoly Commission for action through State trading; and future Labour Governments may well decide not to nationalize any given industry but by owning sufficient shares or appointing directors on certain firms to foster competition within the industry. It is not till policies IV and V are reached that the special Monopoly Commissions or Courts come into full action, either to discourage restrictive practices likely to last or directly to regulate prices. Policy VI, "trust busting" fashionable in America up to 1911 has not been tried in Britain apart from the complete nationalization of monopolistic industries. The mere fact of being a large organization relatively to the whole market, though used as a clue to possible monopoly, has not yet been used as proof against any industrial organization.

CHAPTER IV

PARTICIPATION OF STATE WITH INDUSTRY

§1 *An Introductory Outline*

THE last chapter discussed the way the State defended one party in industrial society from the possible actions of another. Historically the defence of labour from possible exploitation by the capitalist employer was the leading case, but defence also proved necessary for the consumer, the shareholder and the inventor. Defence took several forms, and the generalization seemed to hold that the weakest or least direct form of State intervention was preferred, which would yet be effective. The weaker and less direct forms of State action included the fixing of minimum wages by Wages Councils on which the State participated with employers and workers. Here participation was at first used as a device for achieving the most suitable defence of the more ill-organized workers. Tripartite participation with representatives of the two sides of industry will similarly be found a subsidiary device in gathering information about industry, or in exercising national control over industry as a whole, or even over separate industries.[1]

Participation of the State with industry may, on the other hand, not be a subsidiary device in the defence of some party and may have no other aim than that of industry itself, namely the uninterrupted and efficient production of goods and services. State conciliation, mediation and arbitration to avoid the waste of strikes or lock-outs, immediately come to mind, but many other forms of State participation for the aims inherent to industry itself, have gradually been built up in Britain. It is important to realize their common features as well as their differences. One common feature besides that of aiming at oiling the machinery of negotiation, and making it run smoothly, is the democratic nature of the "tripartite participation" in the sense of government *by* the people. In the last section of this

[1] *See* Chapters V and VI.

chapter, consideration will be given to this aspect, as an aim in its own right.

The State may either merely create, once and for all, a structure, like the Whitley Joint Industrial Councils, combining workers and employers or other parties to industry, and then leave the parties to themselves; or may continue to participate. If the State participates continuously with industrial parties, its nominees may do so either as fellow members on some joint body like the Wages Councils, or, as in the machinery for conciliation, mediation and arbitration, separately at various specific stages in the procedure of discussion and decision.

This chapter will first consider State participation for the smooth running of industry, in particular for avoiding or settling disputes between employers and workers. As part of this consideration the next section (§2) will deal with intervention of the State at certain stages of a dispute, and the following section (§3) with the creation by the State of joint bodies representing employers and workers. At this point it is worth passing in review (§4) the use actually made of the various alternative forms of State participation in settling labour policies. The State now not only cares for the smooth running of industry, however, but takes an interest in greater efficiency, and a further section (§5) must give consideration to the present State participation in industrial "development".

§2 Intervention in Negotiation

The organization for industrial conciliation, mediation and arbitration by the State, initiated in the Conciliation Act of 1896, and extended by the Industrial Courts Act of 1919, is primarily a matter of the timing of State intervention and of the structure, strength and sanctions, with which the State may intervene in the process of negotiation between Employers' Associations and Trade Unions. This form of State intervention is so inextricably connected with Trade Union procedure that most aspects of it have been described in *Trade Unions* and in *Labour* published in the same series as the present book. Here we need only sum up the part played by the State. The various stages at which the State intervenes form the basis of the

distinction between conciliation, mediation and arbitration. Five stages can be distinguished in industrial disputes and negotiation.
  (i) Grievances and initiation of a dispute, possible stoppage.
  (ii) Parties brought together for discussion. Conciliation.
  (iii) Debate and investigation of facts. Courts of Inquiry.
  (iv) Formulation of terms of settlement. Mediation and Arbitration.
  (v) Acceptance of formula. In arbitration but not mediation, acceptance is agreed in advance.

The structures formed by the State for intervening in negotiation are individual persons, boards of persons or "courts" set up either *ad hoc* or permanently. The Act of 1896 allowed the government to appoint a conciliator or arbitrator, the former on application of either party and the latter at the request of both parties to the dispute. Under the Industrial Courts Act of 1919, the Ministry of Labour:

'. . . employs a staff of conciliation officers, whose job it is to help both parties to settle their differences amicably if their advice or assistance is requested, although generally they do not intervene before an attempt has been made to reach a settlement without their help. . . . The Minister of Labour can also appoint single arbitrators or special *ad hoc* Boards of Arbitration, if this course is likely to prove more acceptable to the contesting parties."[1]

Beside conciliation, mediation and arbitration, the Act of 1919 allows the setting up of a Court of Inquiry. While reference to arbitration usually requires the consent of both parties, and reference to conciliation the consent of one, a Court of Inquiry can be, and now usually is, set up by the Minister of Labour on his own initiative, when he considers all other methods of negotiating and settlement to have been exhausted. The Court which usually consists of an independent president and a member from each of two panels representing employers and workers, publishes a report which may merely sum up the contention of each party without making any recommendations; it has no power of enforcement. Recent inquiries have had to consider such diverse questions as the alleged victimization of shop

[1] Flanders, *Trade Unions*. Hutchinson's University Library, 1952, pp. 95–96.

stewards, the general wage level, or wage differentials, involving different conceptions of the "proper" relativities between different occupations, held by a number of separate Trade Unions in the same industry.[1] In answering these questions, State-appointed arbitrators may consider their main duty to be tactical—and tactful. To avoid strikes and to provoke least resistance they may tend to act according to the relative bargaining strengths of the various parties "to award with much unction the lion's share to the lion";[2] or they may act like lawyers on precedent, and try to conserve 'reasonable' relativity patterns and the just price; or they might conceivably consider, rationally, long-term and national economic forces and needs—encouraging, for instance, recruitment to new trades in growing demand or producing goods for export, discouraging old trades no longer wanted. Of the three alternative policies—tactical, "reasonable", or rational, the present trend appears to run somewhere between the tactical and the reasonable, with the rational (and national) frowned upon and openly repudiated. As H. A. Turner puts it, "arbitration must continue in the role in which it has been historically successful—that of an auxiliary to collective bargaining".[3] This respect for collective bargaining was doubly affirmed to be government policy as recently as 1954. The Conservative Minister of Labour was asked in Parliament by the Labour ex-Minister of Labour, if he was "aware that the slightest hint of a suspicion among the workers that arbitration is being tampered with will kill it". The answer was, "There will be no tampering with arbitration as long as I hold my office." Tampering, as Barbara Wootton comments, is here used to describe "the issue of official instructions or guidance to arbitration tribunals",[4] and the policy adopted by both parties can be described very definitely as *laissez collectives faire*.

So much for the stage and structure of intervention; what of its strength? In particular, *are coercive powers ever used*, at least as a last resort?

After debate, information and formulation, the last stage in an industrial dispute is that of agreement, usually taking

[1]*See* Cmd. 9439.
[2]Knowles, *Strikes*, 1952, p. 67.
[3]Wootton, *The Social Foundations of Wage Policy*, 1955, p. 91.
[4]*loc cit.*

the form of acceptance of the formula. Here British practice has occasionally given coercive powers to the State, but the occasion has so far been limited to times of war or the aftermath of war. In 1951 the Industrial Disputes "Order 1376" repealed compulsory arbitration, prohibition of strikes and lock-outs (and penalties for such stoppages) introduced by "Order 1305" in 1940 at the crisis of the Second World War, but kept a certain form of last-resort compulsion. Before the 1939–45 war, under the Acts of 1896 and 1918, State arbitration was the result of application to the Minister of *both* parties to the dispute and the award was therefore almost invariably implemented. The new 1951 order provides for the reporting of disputes by one party only, either representative Trade Unions or Employers' Associations, or individual employers. The Minister then refers the dispute for settlement through joint negotiating machinery, if suitable machinery exists, or take such other steps towards settlement as seem to him expedient. But if the dispute is not thus settled the Minister must refer it to the Industrial Tribunal whose awards on conditions of employment become an implied term of contract between the employers and the workers to whom an award applies, and redress for alleged breach of contract can be sought in the civil courts of justice.

Flanders sums up Order 1376:[1]

"as a new and extremely important experiment in government intervention in the field of industrial relations. It leaves both sides of industry free to resort to "direct action" but provides them with an alternative, if their voluntary arrangements are inadequate or fail to secure a settlement."

A realistic account of the State participation with industry must give some assessment of the comparative frequency with which the State has actually intervened in negotiation in the various ways already indicated. The policy of the Government is to leave wages and working conditions to be settled if possible by negotiation between employers and workpeople or their representative. But State intervention does occur in a certain number of disputes. During 1952, 1953, and 1954, for instance,

[1] *Trade Unions*, 1952, p. 103, to which reference should be made for further details.

320, 353 and 255 disputes were "settled by agreement between the parties following action taken by the Ministry's conciliation officers".[1] Moreover 137, 128 and 114 disputes were settled in the same years through voluntary reference by both sides to the arbitration machinery set up by the State. These settlements were distributed as follows for the three years among the alternative procedures:

Settlements:	1952	1953	1954
Industrial Court (Award issued) . . .	71	64	59
Single Arbitrations (under the Industrial Courts Act) (Award issued)	25	23	18
Civil Service Arbitration Tribunal . . .	33[2]	33	32
Boards of Arbitration appointed . . .	4	4	—
Independent Chairmen as Umpires . .	4	4	5
Total	137	128	114

The disputes reported under the Industrial Disputes Order 1376 numbered, in 1952, 417; and 178 further cases were still in "action" at the beginning of the year. The total of cases under the Disputes Order in 1952 was thus 595 and in 1953 and 1954 the similar totals were 480 and 410. Their histories are worth analysis:

Disputes under the Disputes Order	1952	1953	1954
Referred to the Industrial Disputes Tribunal for arbitration award which will become term of contract	226	202	207
Referred to arbitration machinery under Industrial Courts Acts, 1919 . . .	8	15	1
Settled by reference to joint machinery .	8	3	6
Settled as a resulting action taken by Conciliation Officers	134	135	136
Reports rejected	132	38	6
Still in action at the end of the year . .	87	87	54
Total	595	480	410

[1] Annual Reports of the Ministry of Labour.
[2] 53 in Annual Report, subsequently amended.

Of the disputes referred to the Tribunal a number were settled before the date fixed for the hearing, and in a further number of cases the parties reached agreement on the basis of suggestions made by the Tribunal, and no award was issued.

The first conclusion to be drawn from recent experience is the fairly uniform pattern from year to year; the sharp fall in "reports rejected" is due to the gradual establishment of what constitutes a valid report. A second conclusion is the relatively small proportion of disputes that actually get referred to the final arbitration of the Disputes Tribunal, or indeed to any State-established arbitration or conciliation. For the reader must see State conciliation and arbitration against the background of the total of disputes. Only some disputes result in stoppage, but the stoppages alone were in 1952—1,814; in 1953—1,746; and in 1954—1,994. The relatively small proportion of disputes referred to State conciliation and arbitration compared to the total stoppages (let alone all disputes involving stoppage or not) all ultimately settled, illustrates still further the reluctance to resort to State action, and the bias of industry towards self-determination at least as the first line of approach.

§3 *Joint Industrial Councils and Joint Consultation*

Ranking State action in employer-worker relations according to the strength of State interference—single-handed action without participants coming first, pure *laissez-faire* coming last— the Factory Acts can be placed in the first rank and in the second the Wages Councils. Third would come the intervention in disputes just described; fourth and next to pure *laissez-faire* the mere creation or setting up of Joint Industrial Councils.

The Councils are set up by the State for certain whole industries, but have no State or independent representative sitting on them. Though leaving the employers' and workers' representatives to get on together without further State participation, important tasks appeared to justify the State setting up these Councils under certain conditions. Broadly speaking the agenda for joint consideration were variations on three themes; (i) more efficient utilization of research and of workers' knowledge, experience and invention; (ii) settlement of principles and methods of fixing wages, conditions and security of employment;

TABLE 3: CLASSIFICATION OF LARGER INDUSTRIES[1] BY DEGREE OF STATE PARTICIPATION IN WAGE FIXING

	Per cent of Women among Total Employment[2]	Other Characteristics[3]
1. *No State Participation*		
Brewing	20·3	
Coal Mining	1·9	
Constructional Engineering . . .	8·0	
Cotton—{ Spinning	65·2	}Old established
Cotton—{ Weaving	66·6	} textiles
Engineering	9·0 to 25·0	
Iron Foundries	13·5	
Iron and Steel	8·6	
Marine Engineering	5·1	
Paper	23·4	
Railway Locomotives	5·9	
Ship-building	4·1	
Vehicle-building	14·1 to 14·7	
Wool	56·7	}Old established textiles
2. *Joint Industrial Council; no discussion of wages and hours*		
Brick and Allied { Building Materials .	[4]	Small plants
Brick and Allied { Brick and Fireclay .	.10·0	
Boot and Shoe	51·1	
Printing and Allied { "Other" . . .	39·6	Small plants
Printing and Allied { News . . .	19·8	
3. *Joint Industrial Council; discussion of wages and hours*		
Chemical and Allied { Chemical Dyes . .	21·3	
Chemical and Allied { Explosives and Fireworks .	31·7	
Chemical and Allied { Pharmaceuticals .	57·6	
Electric Cables (and Wires) . .	35·4	
Electricity Supply (3 grades) . . .	11·7	Nationalized
Furniture	25·8	Small plants
Gas	9·5	Nationalized
Hosiery	72·2	
Motor Vehicle Retail & Repair . . .	13·0	Small plants
Pottery	56·4	
Rubber Mfg.	34·8	
Silk (Rayon weaving and silk) . .	39·6	
Sugar Confectionery, Cocoa . . .	63·5	
4. *Wages Councils*		
Baking	41·1	Small plants
Dressmaking	89·6	Small plants
Hollow-ware	54·5	
Laundries	77·7	
Linen and Hemp	65·6	
Paper Box (Cardboard box, etc.) . .	62·5	
Shirtmaking	88·9	
Tailoring	73·1	Small plants

[1]Employing 50,000 or over.

[2]*Ministry of Labour Gazette*, data for June 1954.

[3]Small plants noted if more than 10% of employees in plants employing 10 or less. Average for all mfg. 4·9% (Census of Production 1949).

[4]No separate data.

and (iii) a greater share of responsibility to workers and regular methods of negotiation.

In most industries having these Councils it is the last, the theme of sharing in negotiation, that has, in fact, been developed rather than the technological first theme, and the joint Conciliation bodies voluntarily set up in certain industries, without State intervention, were to a great extent used as models for the State set-up. The creation of the Councils was, in short, justified as filling the gap in the collective bargaining structure in those industries where the workers were not quite able to organize themselves on an equal footing with the employers, but were not so helpless as in the industries where Trade Boards (the present Wages Councils) were set up.

Development of the second theme varied industry by industry. Some councils, like those of the boot and shoe, the paper and printing industries, do not discuss hours and wages, at all.

It is thus possible to draw up a table (3) dividing industries into four successive grades according to the degree of State participation on labour questions:

(1) No State participation, pure *laissez-faire*. Negotiation may occur between industrial parties acting separately; or within a voluntarily set up Joint Conciliation Committee.

(2) Set up by the State of a Joint Industrial Council which does not discuss wages and hours.

(3) Set up by the State of a Joint Industrial Council which does discuss wages and hours.

(4) Set up and continuous participation by the State in a Wages Council.

So many small industries have Wages Councils and Joint Industrial Councils that Table 3 names only those industries that employed in 1954 more than 50,000 workers.

If we are to explain the present and forecast future developments we must look for the sort of factors that characterize industries using one sort of procedure as distinct from industries using other procedures. The main distinctive factors of industries where the State participates more, rather than less, appear to be two: (1) the employment of a high percentage of women;

(2) the prevalence of small plants. Table 3 gives, for each of the larger industries, the percentage of women among the total employed, and notes industries with an unusually high proportion of workers in very small plants. The conclusion may be drawn that a low proportion of very small plants, and higher percentages of men employed, characterize the industries with greater *laissez-faire* and no, or little, State participation. This correlation is no doubt connected with the fact that Trade Unions are less prevalent among women than men and among small firms, and thus collective bargaining without State participation is difficult. Of the five industries that form exceptions to this rule, three textile industries with many women employed yet no State participation, are old established, with women's Trade Unions strongly entrenched; electricity and gas (with few women employed, and few small plants yet having Joint Industrial Councils fixing wages) are nationalized. Nationalized industries, as mentioned in Chapter VI, are particularly inclined to adopt the Joint Industrial Council procedure.

TABLE 4: DEGREES OF STATE PARTICIPATION IN WAGE FIXING AMONG ALL AND AMONG LARGE INDUSTRIES

Procedures in order of strength of State Participation	*Number of Industries*	
	All	Large only (over 60,000) employees)
Direct Negotiation between Trade Union(s) and Employers' Associations: including Joint Industrial Councils without powers to fix wages	45 ⎫ ⎬ 57	15 ⎫ ⎬ 16
Voluntary Conciliation Boards and Joint Wages Committees . .	12 ⎭	1 ⎭
Joint Industrial Councils with power to fix wages	38 ⎫ ⎬ 79	8 ⎫ ⎬ 14
Wages Councils	41 ⎭	6 ⎭
	136	30

If the first two groups of industries in Table 3 are lumped together, some measures can be obtained of the comparative importance of the various forms of State-participation in fixing basic wage rates. The Ministry of Labour publishes at intervals a list of time rates of wages. Taking the list for April 1954, and including the summary of industries covered by Wages Regulation Orders, 136 separate manufacturing industries and public utilities are covered. Table 4 shows that the industries using the two procedures where the State to some extent participates, outnumber industries using the two purely voluntary, Stateless, procedures by 79 to 57.

The industries given in Tables 3 and 4 are of very different size and the very largest industries like engineering, iron and steel, cotton, wool, shipbuilding, are on the whole the industries negotiating directly without State participation. If we take large industries to include all with over 60,000 employees, the second column of Table 4 shows that, in contrast to *all* industries, the large industries contain a higher proportion (16 out of 30 as against 57 out of 136) that use Stateless procedures.

§4 *Review and Analysis of State Participation in Labour Policy*

Different industries have been shown to use radically different procedures and structures for dealing with labour questions. Many use procedures involving coercive sanctions by the State, like the Wages Council method. Other industries use procedures with no or little coercion but involving either continuous State participation or at least structures initially State created, like the Joint Industrial Councils.

Certain connections may be traced between structure, procedure, sanctions and industrial conditions, justifying two or three generalizations and making distinct each of the four main methods: Stateless direct negotiation, negotiation ending in arbitration and mediation, Joint Industrial Councils and Wages Councils.

1. The more the Government participates in bargaining the more are bargains compulsorily enforceable. The wage council method, with a structure giving independent State-appointed members casting votes, ends in an award for a minimum wage which is compulsorily enforced. The decisions of the Joint

Industrial Council procedure with no independent members are not compulsorily enforced.

2. The more strongly the State participates in new awards, the more direct and close is the representation of the industrial parties. The representative members of the Statutory Wages Councils are chosen from within the industry concerned, whereas employers and workers on arbitration tribunals come from outside the industry whose disputes they have to resolve. As Barbara Wootton suggests[1] this difference between the constitution of Wages Councils and that of arbitration tribunals clearly implies a corresponding distinction between the legislative function of the former and the judicial function of the latter. The Wages Council drafts laws for its own industry, whereas the arbitration court gives judgment on matters submitted by others. The choice of industrial arbitrators unconnected with the industries, the merits of whose claims they must judge, is evidently intended as a guarantee that they, like other judges, will be free from bias arising from personal interest.

3. The more strong the voluntary Trade Union organization in an industry the less strong government participation. Strongly organized industries are left to act on their own; weakly organized industries have bargaining organs created for them, like Joint Industrial Councils. Unorganized and perhaps unorganizable industries have the fullest government intervention, in the form of Wages Councils.

What in practice is the measurable effect of each of these different and distinctive methods, taking industry as a whole, upon labour policy? Statistics are provided each year by the Ministry of Labour detailing what proportion of the total changes in wages occurring during the year were due to the different method pursued. The method may be automatic like the sliding scale by which wage-changes are tied to changes in the cost of living index. Apart from this automatic method five alternative procedures are compared: direct negotiation usually by Trade Unions and Employers' Associations, with no State participation whatever; arbitration and mediation which may or may not involve State-appointed arbitrating or mediating persons or bodies of persons; a Joint Industrial

[1] *The Social Foundations of Wage Policy*, 1955, p. 8.

D

Council set up by the State; other bodies set up by voluntary agreement; and finally, where the State intervenes most strongly, as described in the previous chapter, a Wages Council.

TABLE 5: METHODS BY WHICH CHANGES IN RATES OF WAGES WERE ARRANGED 1949–54

Method	Percentages of Total Increase each Year[1]						Unweighted Average 1949–54
	1949	1950	1951	1952	1953	1954	
Under sliding scale[2] .	10·8	7·5[3]	5·5	14·6	19·4	8·3	11·0
Direct Negotiation .	26·1	48·5	45·7	28·2	13·7	45·2	34·6
Arbitration and Mediation . .	12·6	7·5	4·8	12·8	20·0	11·9	11·6
Joint Industrial Councils . .	15·3	15·6	24·4	23·7	9·9	23·3	18·7
Other bodies established by voluntary agreement . .	2·3	1·6	2·1	1·5	1·3	3·7	2·1
Wages Councils and other Statutory Wages Boards .	32·9	19·3	17·5	19·2	35·7	7·6	22·0
Total Increase (£000)	1,074	2,040	6,547	4,426	2,398	3,488	100·0

Table 5 gives the proportion of wage changes due to these alternative methods for each of the years 1949 to 1954. The proportion due to each method varies greatly from year to year, but taking the six-year average, direct negotiation without State participation appears the method used for the greatest amount of changes in wages. Wages Councils, at the other end of the State participation scale, for the next greatest. The use of Joint Industrial Councils, which have powers in wage negotiation, comes third in importance. Before the war of 1939–45 the statistics were not analysed so closely, but for the period 1924–36 there was undoubtedly much greater use of the automatic sliding scale and less use of the "Standing Joint Bodies" in

[1]Source: *Ministry of Labour Gazette*, January following the year specified. The changes in this period were all increases except as noted in 1950.
[2]Some arranged by Joint Industrial Councils, other Standing Joint Councils, Conciliation Boards or Wages Councils.
[3]Representing £154,000. There was also a £20,300 decrease.

which the State participated, such as the Wages Councils and Joint Industrial Councils.

The prevention and cure of disputes resulting in strike or lock-out is, however, the main reason for bringing the State to participate in one way or another with employers and workers in industrial negotiation. Is there any evidence of the comparative effects of different procedures on the number of strikes and man-days lost? When we collate experience from various countries, different industries appear inherently to have different propensities for strikes—mining and docks for instance high; clothing low.[1] It would therefore lead to fallacies to compare the strike experience of, say a Wage Council or a Joint Industrial Council industry with a purely *laissez-faire* industry and to attribute the difference purely to the difference in negotiating procedure. All it is possible to say is that while Britain has been building up her various types of State-participating procedure, the frequency and severity of strikes have been falling and that compared to other industrial countries she reached by 1927-47 a very low level of days lost by stoppage. With a twenty-year annual average of 290 man-days lost per thousand employees she had half the incidence of Belgium, under half that of France, under a third that of Australia and the United States and a fifth that of Sweden. Since 1947, Sweden's strike record has changed from the highest to the lowest on the list, but the relative position of the other countries has altered little, and the United Kingdom shows the lowest figure after Sweden. Indeed, while in most countries the days lost a year in disputes per 1,000 persons employed rose since 1948, in the United Kingdom they just halved—from 290 to 146.[2]

The low British records of days lost by stoppages cannot however be attributed directly to State participation in settling strikes or lock-outs. Relatively few disputes or stoppages, as said earlier, were settled, once they had arisen, by arbitration and conciliation. A summary made for 1924-36 showed only 8½ per cent of all stoppages (and 21 per cent of all persons involved) to have been settled by any sort of conciliation and arbitration—State-participating or not; and between 1937 and

[1]Knowles, *Strikes*, 1952, p. 162.
[2]For details *see International Labour Review*, Nov. 1949; July 1955.

1944 when the analysis was discontinued, the proportion was still lower—6¾ per cent of all stoppages, 7½ per cent of all persons involved.[1] A more probable connection between the low proportion of stoppages in Britain and the British machinery of negotiation with its various forms of State participations, is on the preventive not the curative side. Grievances seem to have been checked before they reached the dispute stage, or disputes before they reach the stoppage stage.

§5 *Participation for Industrial Development*

In the last chapter the State's activities were described in redressing the balance of power between the various parties within industry and defending one party from some of the actions of the others. In this chapter have been described the State's participation with the two main parties to settle their differences. Both these State activities are deviations from the pure policy of *laissez-faire*, but they are not difficult to explain and justify in the light of publicly proclaimed values today. Public opinion now sets a high value on the worker's health and welfare and his standards of living as a consumer. The defence of workers and consumers from exploitation by industry is accepted as a proper activity of the State, no less than preventing or settling disputes, which are likely to diminish national incomes by strikes or lock-outs and that endanger the wealth of the nation.

Deviation from *laissez-faire* represented by the participation of the State with workers' and employers' "collective" organizations is not difficult, either, to explain or justify. It is the obvious policy for composing disputes between the two main industrial parties. At first sight it is less easy to make a case for participation of the State with industrial parties for purposes that are the very root of industry itself. Industry consists in the production of goods and services, and it is the core of the *laissez-faire* doctrine that the individual industrialist is the best judge and exponent of how to produce efficiently at least cost to himself, and that the State should not interfere with the market mechanism.

In spite of this doctrine, we find the State setting up "Development Councils" in various industries between 1948 and 1950 and providing them with some (limited) means to promote and

[1]For details from year to year, *see* Knowles, *op. cit.* p. 37.

undertake activities with the avowed aim "to increase efficiency and productivity in the industry as much as possible, to improve and develop the service that it renders to the community and to enable it to render that service more economically".[1] We also find the State setting up a special Iron and Steel Board to supervise capital development and prices; and Advisory Councils for Industry as a whole and for separate industries—not to mention nationalizing public utility industries outright.

Why is it that the State now takes a hand in the root activity of so many industries? The justification of this radical deviation from *laissez-faire* lies in a confluence of new forces, many already noted in tracing industrial trends.

(i) The industrial revolution did not end in 1820 or 1848 or 1914 but on the contrary is proceeding at an increasing pace with automation as the latest development. To keep up with competition in the home and export market, industrial firms must undertake scientific research or at least have a working knowledge of its latest developments in their field. Research, even communication of working knowledge, requires a staff of experts which the smaller firms cannot afford either to buy or to train up.

(ii) Mechanization and other technological advances, due to scientific discovery and invention, have, moreover, made the large-scale production of a single line of goods very much cheaper per unit than small-scale production. Because of the heavy overhead machine costs, constant regardless of the output, the making of a million standard articles might cost, for instance, only one-twentieth per article that of making only ten thousand. Efficiency and low cost thus require standardization within the industry of a few designs that will sell in large quantities and permit mass production on specialized machines.

(iii) Allocation of overhead costs, not only constant regardless of output but also common to several products, involves difficult cost accounting. A firm without expert advice and comparative costings may make miscalculations serious to itself and to the whole industry.

(iv) Recent analysis, observing, and generalizing from, real facts rather than inferring from theoretical assumptions, has

[1]Proposals for a Development Council for the Jewellery and Silverware Industry, H.M.S.O. 1948.

brought to light the possibility, if not the probability, that the main interests of the top managers of many firms is not always to maximize profits (which as they are not shareholders do not accrue to them) nor yet to increase production and sales by lowering costs and price. And the existence of imperfect monopolistic competition prevents these less expansive firms being driven out of business by expanding firms.

(v) In consequence, the country's competitive power is held to have suffered; and today, when Britain must more than ever export manufactures literally in order to live, public opinion accepts the State taking on some responsibility even for furthering the 'root' efficiency of industry.

(vi) Public opinion, however, is not prepared for the State to take over all industry without the participation of other parties. There is no confidence that universal nationalization would secure the desired efficiency. Moreover, Mill's two objections to State action that are here relevant continue to carry weight. Devolution of State activity and the spontaneous action of people are still valued. Indeed, there seems almost to be a soft spot in public esteem for the "small man" in business. Thus the State is driven to try to co-operate with firms, large and small, in order to provide, for a whole industry, research, or at least up-to-date information, and some large-scale specialized production of standard designs in spite of a small-firm structure.

(vii) In sum, technical and economic development, together with public value-judgments, force the State to interfere at the root of industry, with the very methods of production of the individual firm, but to interfere, only in co-operation with industrial representatives.

Some of the co-operation takes the form of offering services which only the larger firms could perform for themselves— overseas marketing, technical and even social and psychological research, for instance. These services offered to industry will be considered in the next chapter. The forms of State participation for industrial production and efficiency now to be described are those of creating structures within an industry which the State may then either leave employers and workers to run for themselves, or in which the State may continue to participate.

Participation may be of various degrees of strength. The Industrial Development Councils, which the Act of 1947 enabled "the appropriate Minister" to set up for any industry, may be said to favour medium strength in State participation. Once a substantial proportion of the industry agree, the State compels the registration of all traders for the purpose of paying a levy and may compel information to be supplied. In form, at least, it appoints all the members of the Council, after consultation with the appropriate organizations in the industry. A third or rather more of the members represent the producers, another third or rather more the workers, and the remainder are to be independent or expert, one of them usually expert in problems of distribution.

Nineteen "functions" are given in the Act which may be assigned to a Development Council. All of these possible items on the agenda were recommended in one or other of the reports of the Working Parties set up by Sir Stafford Cripps in a score of industries, and most of them were suggested in most of the reports—which indeed bore a certain family likeness. One or two types of recommendation of many of the working party reports, notably the provision of new capital equipment, did not materialize, however, in any duty, officially assigned to the Development Councils. Other procedures have been adopted for control over capital and will be inquired into later.

All the Working Parties suggested setting up some kind of structure or structures to carry on activities for the industry as a whole, whether it was design centres or "export associations" or a "production efficiency organization". Whether one or more such structures were to be set up, the activities the Working Parties expected them to perform were fairly similar for most of the industries and became one or other of the nineteen functions assigned to the Development Council in the Act of 1947. We need not list these nineteen particular functions since no industry, where a Council was set up, in fact pursued them all, but they fall into five groups of related activities.

(i) "Promoting or undertaking" research, or inquiry. Research may cover matters ranging widely—from industrial psychology, through methods of production management and labour utilization to marketing arrangement and consumer research.

(ii) Promoting training and arrangements for encouraging the entry of persons into the industry.

(iii) Safety, amenities and welfare of labour.

(iv) Promoting the production and marketing of standard products, the improvement of design, the definition of trade description, the registration of trade-marks, and the development of the export trade.

(v) Promoting the improvement of accounting and costing practice, in particular the formulation of standard costings, and undertaking the collection and formulation of statistics.

State-created structures to participate in the first three types of activity have already been encountered (particularly as part of the duties of the Joint Industrial Councils) and the distinctive activities projected for the Development Councils come under the last two headings. Few small firms pretend to engage in research, or to promote training (except through apprenticeship) or to make arrangements for their labour supply. Nor do many of them promote amenities beyond what is required by Factory Acts or Joint Industrial Councils. Hence the admission— by default—of some State interest. But they did expect to "know their own business" in production and marketing, designing and accounting. The creation of Development Councils was, in short, a new incursion of the State into the very roots of industrial activity and business behaviour.

In the years immediately following their foundation under the influence of Sir Stafford Cripps, the Development Councils did not themselves develop as had been hoped. Only in four industries were such councils ever started, and in two of these, clothing and the jewellery and silverware trade, were soon abandoned. The Cotton Board was a reconstitution of earlier organizations, so that the Furniture Council is the unique survivor of the creations of the 1947 Act. In the first five years of its existence the Furniture Council has carried out in practice many of the duties assigned to it on paper, notably the survey and organization of courses of training in management as well as craftsmanship, the testing of the "performance" of certain designs with a view to a voluntary marking scheme incorporating certain standards, comparative costing, and the communication of new technical information to its members, partly financed by the (Government) Department of Scientific and Industrial Research. Here the aim of the Council is admittedly to "assist manufacturers with particular reference to small and medium-sized firms . . . to raise the standard of efficiency".[1]

The almost immediate failure of all Development Councils, except one or two, may have been due to tactical errors in the method of their introduction. Perhaps, however, this "medium strength" participation by the State is a compromise impossible to pull off. Sir Stafford Cripps was indeed contemplating a stronger State admixture. The main cause of failure was the objection of employers to outsiders like the independent members, and even Trade Union officials, sitting on the Council, and to the payment of a levy compulsory *on all*, even though the agreement of only a "substantial number" of them was needed for the Council to be started. If it proves true that the present "middle" position is untenable, the strength of State participation may be either increased or diminished.

In several industries State participation exists which is weaker than in the Development Council pattern. An industry may have a *Joint Advisory* Committee or Council. Such a committee has no statutory powers to call for information or to impose a levy for limited purposes and may or may not contain independent members. The State's activity is confined to setting up the Committee and possibly appointing the independent members, if any. Examples of such bodies occur in branches of the engineering industry (gauges and tools, machine tools, motor manufacturing, heavy electrical plant) and the shipbuilding industry. Many of these advisory committees are planned for a two-way traffic in advice, and industrialists' advice to the State government is often the more important direction; the committees are, in fact, largely a device for devolution of government. In addition to an advisory committee for general purposes of efficiency and development, an industry may have for special purposes a research association, an export corporation, and a recruitment and training council on all of which the workers can be represented.

The State has helped to set up these special organizations

[1] 2nd Annual Report, 1950.

D°

covering a whole industry (the research associations, for instance, through the Department of Scientific and Industrial Research) and often helped to finance them, but nothing more. These organizations present, in fact, a considerably weaker pattern of State participation than the Development Councils, possibly the minimum that could be called participation.

One industry, however, exhibits a State participation in its development and economic policies stronger than the Development Council pattern, namely Iron and Steel. Here an Iron and Steel Board for the "general supervision" of the industry had been set up in 1946 and was increased in strength after the vicissitudes of nationalization and then denationalization. In the present phase (1956) of private operation of the industry, the participation of the State in the general supervision deviates notably from the Development Council structural procedure at four main points.

1. All the members of the Board are nominated by the State on qualifications other than specifically representing the employers or workers concerned.

2. The activities of the Board include reviewing the productive capacity of the industry and arrangements for providing and distributing raw materials and fuel.

3. The Board are empowered, after consultation with the Industry and with appropriate representative organizations (employers' and workers' organizations, both in the iron and steel and consuming industries) to fix maximum home prices, and producers are obliged not to exceed any prices so fixed— an obligation enforceable by civil proceedings. And the Minister is empowered, after consultation with the Board, to make an order directing the Board to fix the maximum price.

4. All major development schemes must be submitted for the approval of the Board, and the Board may refuse consent if, after consultation with the company concerned and the appropriate representative associations the scheme appears "seriously prejudicial to the efficient and economic development of production facilities". This State participation in capital development is positive as well as negative: the Board is to consult with the Industry and others to secure the carrying out of developments.

The question whether State participation for efficiency and development with any one industry will, like the Iron and Steel example, be stronger than the Development Council type, or weaker, is likely to be determined by a number of characteristics of an industry. Determining factors are how far the industry is, like Iron and Steel, basic to the whole economy and has a relatively simple price structure. Another factor is the existing voluntary organization of the industry. The industry may have one predominating firm or, like the Iron and Steel industry, have one or more strong associations and federations among its firms, with committees or sub-committees exercising special duties of interest to the whole industry. At the other end of the scale, an industry may be particularly unorganized, each firm, however small, relying on its own resources for technical knowledge, training and design. What is curious at first sight is that government participation has been applied in industries at each end of the scale, either highly organized or hardly organized at all, rather than in industries middling organized. Possibly there is some "golden mean" of organization which public opinion considers ideal and thus to be completely let alone by the State—a mean, yielding mutual services without risk of monopoly.

Which way State participation for efficiency and development will move in the future cannot be foretold. The question is not as yet a political party issue, though it might become so, and organization is more likely to be affected by economic events and trends than by party fortunes. If certain British industries are found to be losing ground in the export trade or on the home market, and seem unable or unwilling to help themselves, some sort of continuing State participation is likely to be instituted, particularly if the existence of the small firm continued to be valued by public opinion.

Here several curious paradoxes are involved which make prophecy particularly difficult. The "small men" are often the chief antagonists of State participation, particularly if they must compulsorily contribute a levy to maintain the State-created joint body. Yet this body may in some industries be standing between many small men and their extinction. The Conservative is, on the whole, the party against State interference, although it is the party in favour of the small business man whom State interference would benefit. Finally, Trade Unions support the Labour Party and its ideology of State planning (and do not have to pay levies!), and are therefore inclined to favour State participation; but they are not keen on helping to keep the "petty bourgeois" small man alive!

So far the participation of the State has been observed in developing separate industries. The State also has a care for the efficiency and development of industry as a whole. This care is explicable either as part of the general control exercised by the State *over* industry and the economy generally, discussed in a later chapter; or explicable (and discussed in the following section) as part of a democratic and devolutionary trend in affairs of State, which largely depends on the organization of public opinion.

§6 *State Participation and Democracy*

Carrying on production by preventing or settling disputes and stimulating development is no doubt the primary aim explaining State participation with industry. But a secondary aim is observable, that of introducing more democracy in industry, particularly more control by the worker. Ever since the time of Ruskin, observers of industry have been prone to contrast the growing democracy of political England with the lack of democracy, indeed the waning democracy, of industrial England. Where the small factory and firm prevailed there were more independent entrepreneurs and, within each small factory or firm, there was likely to be more camaraderie particularly if the boss or "gaffer" worked alongside his "help".[1] But in one industry after another the size of factory and firm was, and is, growing. Even by 1935 (when the Census of Production first provided accurate data), a majority of workers in most of the larger industries were employed in large factories; seven of the 21 largest British industries (motors, iron and steel, electrical machinery, silk and artificial silk, shipbuilding, newspapers and cocoa) had an absolute majority of workers in factories employing over 500; another six (wool, cotton-spinning, iron foundries, shoes, pottery and paper) had over 60 per cent of their workers in factories employing over 200.[2] Many of these factories were

[1]Florence, *Logic of British and American Industry*, 1953, pp. 274–6.
[2]*op. cit.* pp. 22–9.

under the common ownership of a single firm, so that still greater proportions of workers were in *firms* employing over 200 or 500.

In these large-plant industries the worker is liable to feel particularly like a mere cog, doomed to repetition and routine. Above him towers a bureaucratic superstructure or hierarchy apparently enmeshed in red-tape, through which he feels unable to communicate.

Joining a Trade Union is likely to be his first positive reaction, but though the Webbs called their book which analysed the Trade Union Movement *Industrial Democracy* the movement did not satisfy those who by "democracy" meant workers controlling, or at least identifying themselves with industry. Ruskin, as early as 1862, saw an "apparent anomaly".

"It is easy to imagine an enthusiastic affection existing among soldiers for the colonel. Not so easy to imagine an enthusiastic affection among cotton-spinners for the proprietor of the mill. A body of men associated for purposes of robbery (as a Highland clan in ancient times) shall be animated by perfect affection, and every member of it be ready to lay down his life for the life of his chief. But a band of men associated for purposes of legal production and accumulation is usually animated, it appears, by no such emotions, and none of them are in anywise willing to give his life for the life of his chief."[1]

In Ruskin's day economists certainly paid too little attention to the satisfaction of the producers' emotions. In the last chapter of his *Theory of Political Economy*, for instance, Jevons thus states "the great problem of Economy . . . given, a certain population with various needs and powers of production, in possession of certain lands and other sources of materials; required, the mode of employing their labour so as to maximize the utility of the produce". J. A. Hobson comments, "it seems curious that (Jevons) should have failed to add the words 'and so as to minimize the disutility of producing it' ".[2]

Later in the history of economics, Marshall corrected this omission by drawing attention to the "real costs" of labour and the trend of the social sciences is now to stress the possible

[1] *Unto this Last*, Everyman Edition, p. 122.
[2] *Free Thought in the Social Sciences*, 1926, p. 92.

values to be gained and lost in the course of work as no less important than the value of consumer satisfaction and consumer sovereignty. Industrial psychology and industrial sociology, particularly the experiments of Elton Mayo, have demonstrated the producer's feeling for status, security and social approbation in his work, and the informal controls he exercises over production. The fame and the gang nexus have to be reckoned with, beside the cash nexus.

The trend of academic theory is matched by the changes in the ideologies of the workers themselves and of the Trade Unions that have, since Ruskin's day, so immensely grown in power. Particularly round the period of the First World War (as recounted in Chapter II), many Trade Unionists adopted a syndicalist outlook that would keep State activity at a minimum. In practice this meant Trade Unions (*syndicats* in French) taking charge, though the reconciliation of syndicalism and faith in State control, developed in Britain as Guild Socialism, admitted that the State might have to participate so far as owning the industrial equipment. With the outbreak of the Russian Revolution and its Workers' Councils or Soviets, a move towards workers' control gathered force, and Lloyd George's Government looked for a State-sponsored scheme, "for securing that industrial conditions affecting the relations between employers and workmen shall be systematically reviewed by those concerned".

The original scheme of Joint Industrial Councils was devised by the 1916–19 Reconstruction Committee's sub-committee with Mr. J. H. Whitley, the Speaker of the House of Commons, in the chair. This Whitley Committee envisaged not merely a Joint Council for each whole industry, as already described, but a hierarchy based on District Councils and Works Committees, topped by an Economic Parliament. Accounts had been published of Committees on which sat workers' as well as employers' representatives in a number of model factories, and it was thought that, with a little priming and oiling by the State, many more might be organized. It was realized then, and has since been abundantly demonstrated by industrial sociologists, that the smaller the group concerned and the more personal the impact, the more likely was a high proportion of its members to "become involved" and each member to identify his own and the group's interest. To have life, industrial democracy and the discussion of personal grievances and matters of personal impact must be based not on the whole industry but on the unit of the workshop or factory, and in larger factories perhaps on the unit of the department or primary working group. Identification of interests is important not only for the sake of democracy, but because the technical requirements of modern industry require adaptability and co-operation in the labour force. To cover the fixed overhead costs of machinery in a factory, for instance, multiple shifts have to be worked at hours inconvenient to many workers. British Trade Unions, however, mostly dating from the era of small workshops, are organized by whole industries or crafts, not by factories; and on the workers' side, to satisfy the need for factory-based organization, shop stewards appeared.

The Whitley scheme, likewise, failed in its lower, factory, rungs so vital for democracy and for adjustment to technical needs; and in the Second World War a new State-sponsored drive was undertaken to organize Joint Production Committees in factories, and Joint Pit Committees in mines. In these committees public opinion hoped that greater enthusiasm would be generated for the many factory and mine adjustments needed in pursuing the war's objectives. It was realized that the semiskilled operatives, reduced by modern mechanization to performing one small routine operation hundreds of times, sometimes thousands of times a day, would want to know what exactly the job was for and where it fitted into the firm's production and the whole war effort.

Accordingly, the State government tried to stimulate the establishment of joint consultation within single factories, not only to deal with labour questions but also with questions of technical development. Setting up these committees was fairly easy in State-owned plants, like the Royal Ordnance Factories, and not too hard where the State was the only, or the chief, customer as in privately owned works making munitions of war.

A model constitution of a joint production committee was drawn up in 1942 for application to the Royal Ordnance Factories. Management and workers were to be equally represented and the stated object was the "regular exchange of views between the management and the workers on matters relating to the improvement of production, to increase efficiency for this purpose and to make recommendation thereon". The Committees were not considered necessary, except by mutual desire, in establishments employing less than 150 work-people. Clearly informal democratic exchange of views is more difficult the larger the factory, hence the logic of formal exchanges in a committee where a two-way traffic in communication comes naturally and individual persons on either side get to know one another.

The State, in short, participates with employers and workers up to a certain middle point. Two questions are therefore relevant: why does the State participate as much as it does; why does it not participate more? The answer to the first question is that the State participates to prevent, or settle, certain stoppages and also to get a more democratic procedure started in industry.

The answer to the second question is that democracy as conceived in Britain both by employers and workers still implies the *minimum* of State control. The past and present attitudes of industrialists are well put by Tillyard:

"The typical employer of a generation or two ago had a positive feeling in favour of going his own way and managing his business as he pleased, but he also had a negative feeling expressed in the phrase that he was "agin the Government". The positive feeling has been modified by his association with other employers, but that association has, if anything, strengthened his feeling that Government interference in the management of a business is a mistake. Individually he feels himself the equal, and generally the superior, of any Government official, and in association with his fellow employers that feeling is developed."[1]

This view of the State in the eyes of industry has been likened by an American psychologist[2] to the "father figure" present in the unconscious of a son fighting to become head of the family himself. Its effect is to limit acceptance of the offer of participation by postponing and by weakening intervention.

State policy is to postpone intervention until first all local

[1]Tillyard, *The Worker and the State*, 1923, pp. 43–4.
[2]Lauterbach, *Man, Motives and Money*, 1954, p. 73.

voluntary machinery has failed, then all district and national machinery has failed, and even then to participate to only a mild degree, as conciliator rather than mediator, mediator rather than arbitrator. As Mary Follett puts it,[1] both arbitration and conciliation usually end in a compromise, but in arbitration "you have an adjudicated compromise"; in conciliation "an internally adjusted compromise, a compromise to which both parties agree, to which both parties have perhaps contributed". Each party to arbitration puts up a case to the arbitrator in the forensic manner of the law courts. Under the conciliation procedure parties come in the attitude that the other party may have something to say that is worth hearing—an attitude more responsible and democratic and fit for integrated self-government, and often more likely to reach the truth, than forensic contentiousness scoring debating points and denigrating opponents' witnesses. Besides the preference of conciliation over arbitration, *laissez-faire* also appears in the State's encouragement and creation of joint bodies where workers' and employers' representatives from a given factory or industry meet together, without the presence of independent State appointed members; and appears in the State's confining participation so often to providing information.

The State's activity in publishing information will be discussed later. Here it need only be remarked that the growing use of a Court of Inquiry with its official report without sanctions to enforce its recommendations is in line with the employers' and the workers' identification of *laissez-faire* with democracy. The reports bring the case dispassionately before the bar of public opinion, which is often not well served by newspaper accounts of the causes of disputes; but it leaves public opinion to influence the industrial parties without formal State action.

The State's self-denying ordinance limiting its participation does, however, depend for success upon a certain sweet reasonableness on the part of the employers and workers and also on a wide area of agreement in fundamental attitudes. In Britain practical reasonableness as against doctrinal intransigence is carried further than most industrial countries, and there is the blessed adjective "fair" to conjure with. The notion of "fairness"

[1]*Dynamic Administration*, 1941, p. 233.

is partly connected with sporting activities in which all classes join as in "fair play", where conditions are equal; partly connected with compromise as in "fairly" good—not quite the perfect best but perhaps the best attainable in the interests of all. And it is agreement on norms of fair play and fair shares that makes collective bargaining between opposing interests "work" with the minimum of State participation.

The word "work", however, should perhaps be modified to "tick-over". For agreement by employer, worker and State on "fair" policies will do no more than maintain a certain *status quo*. Yet the economic situation, particularly of a country such as Britain, dependent on other countries for its food and raw materials, is continuously changing. Man-power has to be switched from one industry to another according to export opportunities or the innovation of a new process. This switching may require relative wages higher than customary to be paid in the industries to be expanded, less than customary in the industries to be contracted. Such a change in relativities will certainly be hailed as "unfair", and worker and employer participation in wage fixing will find it "unreasonable".

Should the State in its participation not exercise some influence, issue some directive, for national efficiency? To judge from the majority of authorities, no. *Laissez-faire* remains the basic rule, and the opposition of the traditional "reasonable" to the "rational",[1] haunts State action over the whole national economy. Here our concern is with the democratic aims of a threefold participation in the government of industry by employers, workers and the State, and we can only note the risk that the plan of industrial "self-government" by the people may end in a medieval stereotype of just prices, fair relativities and fixed relationships, and even a hierarchy of classes, quite unsuited to the fluid conditions of the modern world.

[1]See above, p. 89.

CHAPTER V

STATE INFORMATION, SERVICES AND PALLIATIVES

§1 *Introductory Distinctions*

THREE further relations of the State to industry form part of national policy today. All of them have a wider application than industry alone, but the present analysis will be confined to the industrial implications. The distinction between these relations is adequately expressed by the operative prepositions about, for and against; but an additional distinction is that normally the information which is published is ABOUT a whole industry or a general problem, the service offered is FOR an individual person or firm, and the palliative provided is AGAINST the hazard to an individual person only. There is an apparent no-man's land, or rather a both-man's land, between information and service wherever the State offers an individual person a service of information, for instance, when an employment exchange informs a worker about a job. This is primarily however a service FOR a firm or individual and not a general publication of information, and will be taken accordingly.

The three distinct State relations considered in this chapter will be discussed in the following three sections. Each section begins with a summary description of the structure, procedure and devices adopted in Britain by the State and (the transition being marked by a break in the text) follows with an assessment of the aims of the policy, the reasons for State rather than private activity, and the achievement of aims or failure of achievement.

§2 *Information About Industry*

State activity in providing information about industry has already been mentioned frequently. Collecting information must always form part of an efficient State government, as

William the Conqueror understood when he ordered the Domesday Book to be compiled; but the characteristic of democratic governments in a free society is that information is disseminated to the public, so that the public may reach an informed opinion on which to base its judgments. The information that is published by the State is normally collected, sifted and drawn up by some official body: either by a body appointed *ad hoc* and composed mainly of members of the public or officials of State, such as Royal Commissions or departmental or inter-departmental committees, so prominent from time to time as precursors of legislation; or, like much of the information about industry in official periodicals (e.g. the *Board of Trade Journal* and the *Ministry of Labour Gazette*), or a Ministry's annual reports and occasional papers, may be just the routine activity of Government departments. In a free society these State publications are subject to uncensored public criticism by private citizens and bodies and are, indeed, only one set of publications about industry among the many issuing from private hands—daily and weekly newspapers, learned journals and books, reports of Trade Associations and other such bodies.

In one form of information about industry and the economy generally the State is now pre-eminent—the publication of statistics.

"Fifty years ago there were no production statistics outside a few staples, such as coal, pig iron and steel. International trade was reasonably well covered, and estimates could be made of the British consumption of commodities such as cotton, wool and wheat, of which a good part passed through the ports. The basic financial and fiscal statistics were published; wage rates were known for selected trades, and unemployment figures could be obtained from Trade Union returns. Indices of wholesale prices were available, and there was some scattered information about retail prices, mainly of food. General "activity" could be seen reflected in the railway returns, the shipping clearances, or the bank clearings. But the items of this rudimentary statistical system were often of an unsatisfactory kind; . . .

By 1939 things were substantially better; the *Guide to Current Official Statistics of the United Kingdom*, published annually from 1922, gives an idea of the wealth of information available. But the user was still faced by difficulties of inadequate coverage, of varying classification, and so on, and many areas of statistics now familiar were hardly developed at all. In the field of industrial production, for instance, the Board of Trade index of 1935 contained about 85 series; the Central Statistical Office index of 1952 contains 1,300. In 1939 national income statistics of a simple kind had been worked out by a few private investigators: in 1952 the extensive and complex information given in the National Income White Papers draws from the resources of almost every Government department and forms a considerable part of the work of the Central Statistical Office. . . .

This change has not been uniform; some types of statistics have been developed almost to excess, while for others there may have been some retrogression. The growth of statistical information was, in fact, haphazard. Much of it came into being in response to some special administrative need, perhaps short-lived . . ."[1]

The aim of publishing information by the State about industry has been indicated as enlightening public opinion and forming the basis for successful democratic government able to frame policy and cope realistically with facts when the facts are known. Knowledge of the facts of a situation is also necessary in the administration of the State itself. An essential ingredient, as we shall see, of planning is that the existing situation, and the "performance" and effects upon the situation of new plans, be exactly measured. In short, statistical survey and statistical control are demanded by efficient administration.

Reasons why the State collects and publishes information about industry thus arise from the *demand* side; and an important, if not the main, demand for such information and statistics comes from government administrators or from bodies with which the government participates, such as Trade Unions and Employers' Associations. So urgently did State departments need information during the war of 1939–45 that a governmental "social survey" was set up, to which the departments could delegate investigation of particular problems that faced them. These problems might arise within the administration of government such as the saving of expenditure in producing telephone directories, if some subscribers were prepared to go without; might arise in the co-operation of private individuals with the government, such as problems of road safety; or might arise

[1]Carter and Roy, *British Economic Statistics*, 1954, pp. 1–2.

purely in private behaviour which was, however, of public interest, like industrial productivity. Two or all three of these sources of demand may account for the deviation from *laissez-faire*. In adjusting wage-rates to the cost of living, for instance, whether by bilateral action of employers and wage-earners or by trilateral participation of State nominees with the two interested parties, an index of retail prices must clearly be published officially, by the State.

Even where the demand for information is not official or even semi-official, such as the demand from Universities for teaching and research data, or the demand from business, the requirement of reliability and freedom from bias and of comprehensiveness makes State collection and publication of information the only alternative. But it may well be asked how far official collection and publication of information has achieved the satisfaction of this unofficial demand.

One complaint from the consumers of State publications is of the lag that occurs so often between the events observed and their appearance in print. This delay is an almost universal complaint from industrial organizations about the Census of Production; but it is improbable that such a large and complicated inquiry could have its delivery date very sharply put forward, if it is to be reliable and comprehensive. The Population Census has cut down the time lag by publishing a 1 per cent sample. Production, however, is too heterogeneous for all but its broadest outlines to be thus drastically sampled. The failure to satisfy business demand probably lies deeper—in the nature of the demand itself. As the *Economist* has put it:

"No real explanation has been offered why British industry apparently differs from industry in other countries in making so little use of the statistical treasure-house provided by periodic and properly conducted census of the economy. These returns . . . should be valuable to any business. Many industries maintained that their own trade associations collected and circulated adequate figures. But such figures are not always comprehensive; they depend on how wide is the association's membership, and they are not necessarily available to industries and companies that are not association members. They are trade secrets."[1]

[1] Oct. 30th, 1954. p. 402.

Confusion apparently exists, in the minds of the business consumer of statistics, between continuous following up of trends and fluctuations in prices, volume of production, employment, stocks, sales, incomes, etc., useful for forecasting and for immediate business decisions; and the periodic survey of industrial structure undertaken by a Census. Both must be as reliable as possible. But while the continuous follow-up must be up to date, the periodic census either acts as an audit on the correctness of the continuous follow-up, or deals with the more permanent structure of the economy such as the size, location or integration of establishments. This information about economic structure, comprehensive, but not necessarily up to the minute, though less important to single firms, is vital to all industrial reorganization, as in planning for war-time or replanning for peace or, as we shall see (p. 159) in deciding which industries to nationalize.

A possible consequence of State information, more serious than mere delay in meeting the demand for the truth, the whole truth and nothing but the truth, is the risk of political bias. The danger of getting untruths or half-truths is largely avoided in a society where free discussion and criticism is allowed and where a civil service has been built up with professional standards. But vigilance and some education is required if the public is to obtain the whole truth.

Reasons why the State and not private enterprise collects and publishes information about industry also arise from the *supply* side. Much of the information is about the State's own part in industry, details of which only the State can supply. For democratic government the public must be informed about State plans and administrative performance. White papers, the central office of information and departmental public relations officers, all serve this aim; and much of the statistics officially published come from the records necessarily collected in the course of administering government departments, for instance the number of workers registered at the employment exchanges or the expenditure on various items by public authorities.

Where the information is mainly at the demand of private persons and about the activities of private industrial organizations, it might be thought that, since State publications are sold at a price, private non-official publication would do as well. This *laissez-faire* view ignores the fact that no organization could supply the complete information so necessary to avoid bias, without the powers of coercion reserved to the State. The Census of Production, for instance, if compiled voluntarily would not get all firms to answer, nor even a random sample. The firms answering voluntarily would tend to be firms of particular goodwill, or firms pleased with their particular records.

§3 *Services for Industry*

The State provides a wide variety of services to industrial firms and individuals in industry through departments of State, and also through institutions specially set up and through local authorities.

The department chiefly involved is the Ministry of Labour. In its Annual Reports consecutive chapters describe the "services" of the Ministry: the Employment Services, Youth Employment, Training for Employment and in the Skills of Supervision, and Resettlement of Disabled Persons. The Employment Services include the work of the employment exchanges for labour where in 1954, for instance, as many as 3,095,000 placings were effected, about 14 per cent of the total persons in civil employment, with 338,000 vacancies unfilled; and also include the work of the appointments service for "occupations" of a professional, administrative, managerial, technical or scientific character. The Youth Employment Service includes placing young people under 18, advising them on careers through "vocational guidance" (mainly in school hours) and the issue of *Choice of Careers* booklets, and then following up their progress at work after they are placed. These Youth Employment Services deal in hundreds of thousands: in 1954, for instance, 449,000 boys and girls were placed in employment, 492,000 were given vocational guidance (some of it perhaps rather perfunctory), and 315,000 boys and girls replied in writing or came to meetings in reply to inquiries as to their progress; other follow-up action was taken in 199,000 cases. Further classes of service by the Ministry of Labour apply only to a limited number. Training for Employment was empowered by Acts of 1944 and 1948 to supply vocational training for disabled persons and to supplement skilled labour in short supply in industries of particular national importance. The Resettlement service provides courses of industrial rehabilitation and training, assesses the individual capacity of the disabled, selects their employment carefully, supplies physical aids where necessary and places them either in ordinary employment (employers of twenty or more persons are required to employ disabled persons to the extent of 3 per cent of their total staff) or in special sheltered conditions. These sheltered conditions are provided in almost a hundred factories under a public company formed in 1945 (with the title of Remploy) by the Minister of Labour. The factories work largely on Government contracts.

The Ministry of Labour thus serves industry by helping to find labour, and man firms up more efficiently. Other State departments as well as the Ministry serve by helping in the more efficient supply of the other factors of production besides labour: risk capital and finance, management and technical know-how.

State services helping in the supply of capital and finance are confined narrowly to the guarantee of payment for exports by the Export Credits Guarantee Department organized in its present form in 1928, and to subsidies for organizations created to finance either particular industries or small and medium firms generally. The Board of Trade has made large advances amounting to over 9 million pounds by 1954 to the National Film Finance Corporation for investment in and loan to film producers. State help in the financing of small and medium-sized firms generally takes the form of Bank of England participation with the Joint Stock banks or investment and insurance companies in special corporations, such as the Finance Corporation for Industry or, for the smaller firms, the Industrial and Commercial Finance Corporation. These corporations will make medium and long-term loans to industrial firms, especially for new development.

State services for technical "know-how" and industrial management come today through a variety of government departments or of institutions specially set up, usually with a Council of leading private citizens of some relevant experience. The Department of Scientific and Industrial Research undertakes and subsidizes research in the physical—and recently some social—sciences. The Ministry of Labour acts almost as a consultant through its Personnel Management and Advisory Service. The Board of Trade has set up and financed, in part, a Council of Industrial Design and a British Institute of Management, to raise the standards current in private industries.

Where a government department is providing the services to industry rather than a semi-independent State-aided Council, it is careful to consult representatives of the interested industrial parties and also independent experts, largely through standing Joint Advisory Councils. This consultation applies especially to the problems of particular types of worker in industry. The Ministry of Labour, for instance, has at headquarters the following advisory councils or committees:

The National Advisory Council on the Employment of Older Men and Women.

Women's Consultative Committee.

National Advisory Council on the Employment of the Disabled.

National Youth Employment Council.

Locally the most important committees advising on services are perhaps the Local Employment Committees which bring the Employment Exchanges into close touch with employers and workers in the areas they serve. Membership follows the usual pattern of workers' and employers' representatives with independent "additional" members, some with special knowledge or experience, nominated by local authorities.

Local authorities provide (with central State subsidies) the main education of youth and technological and commercial education of adults; moreover the committees who are in charge of this education are committees of democratically elected Councils. Participation of local authorities in the procedure for providing State service for industry is thus in keeping with the pattern of a demo-technocratic consultative "surround" for the State administration.

Why does the State perform these services for industry rather than letting industry itself do the work, and why in the particular forms just described?

The main reason is that the services provided by the State for industry, unlike its publication of information, are normally not paid for by the consumer but paid out of national taxes or local rates. They are services which have been found not to be in demand if a price is charged covering the full cost and which therefore private enterprise will not supply, however widely the service is judged of national importance. The leading case is that of education supplied free by the State because many parents could not or would not keep their children at school the length of time judged desirable. In industry this gap—if it is not a void—between national need and market supply occurs in technical and management education. In the middle ages, apprenticeship with an existing firm supplied the need, but today, with less traditional needs and almost universal specialization between and within firms, manual skills and administrative techniques must largely be taught by local education authorities in the technical and commercial colleges they have developed since the Education Act of 1902. The needs of modern industry even require that applied sciences and the tools of higher management—accounting, statistical analysis, commercial law, administrative principles, industrial economics—be taught at Universities with State subsidies allocated by the University Grants Committee.

Most general and technical education is today a free service performed, or at least subsidized, by central and local State authorities; but other types of services for industry are provided by the State only in exceptional situations, the bulk of the service being left to private enterprise. The reason adduced for such exceptional State interference is usually that some "gap" has appeared in the market mechanism for serving some aim growing in national importance.

The realization in recent years that Britain must depend for its prosperity and especially the volume of its exports on human wits rather than natural materials like coal, has been confronted with the suspicion that in management skills Britain lags behind other countries. The State has out of its tax revenue provided grants for this reason to the British Institute of Management (for a limited period), and to the Council of Industrial Design. Both were set up for improving the standards of performance by business firms, which, unaided by the State, generally seemed slow in their adjustment to new situations.

A specific risk consequent on State services for management is that certain techniques favoured by the State will, thanks to free service or subsidization, gain precedence over other and possibly better techniques. The Council of Industrial Design, or its nominees, select exhibits for showing at home and abroad and there is always the danger in such State control that one school of taste will gain an undue prestige, as exemplified by the privileges of the Royal Academy. However, if no move, or only feeble moves, are made by private enterprise to improve its management technique, or its industrial design, then the market mechanism has clearly failed. The State may well fill the gap, being careful, however, not to set up a monopoly of types of technique or taste, but to follow up critically the consequences of its action, for instance the effect of exhibitions on sales. The failure of the market mechanism is clear in education for management when compared with the United States. Though fifty years ago England was as early in the field as America with a liberal University degree course oriented towards a business career, British business did not then see its value as (to judge from Productivity teams[1]) it does now. Though a few Universities followed in the footsteps of Birmingham, the B.Com. degree never took hold as the American B.Com. or B.A. in Business Administration. Today, through the University Grants Committee, the State may be prepared to help finance courses in Commerce or Administration which private business, not appreciating their effect on recruits to business, failed to support.

So much in justification of State services to that increasingly important factor of production, management. The other two main factors in industry, labour and capital, as already described, have not been neglected by State services either, and for much the same reasons: gaps, if not voids, in the market mechanism of supply and demand.

The main gap left by employers and Trade Unions in the efficient organization of labour is lack of provision for its smoother mobilization for industrial needs and demands, and it was for this reason that the State set up in 1909 the labour (later called employment) exchanges with the avowed purpose of

[1] e.g. Anglo-American Council on Productivity. Report on Education for Management, 1951.

reducing "frictional" unemployment. During the great depression of 1929–35 the State also offered free transport to help move labour from areas of low to areas of less low employment. The servicing of capital which the State undertakes for industry is confined mainly to the general financing of the *small* firm and to the export activities of all firms. The reason again is a gap in the existing market mechanism because private enterprise was apparently unwilling to accept uncertain risks. The Committee on Finance and Industry with Lord Macmillan in the chair and Keynes as a member reported in 1931 that facilities were available in the London Capital Market for short-term loans financing trade and commerce and for the issue of foreign bonds "as distinguished from the financing of British industry". In "home investment", as it was represented to the Committee,

"great difficulty is experienced by the smaller and medium-sized businesses in raising the capital which they may from time to time require, even when the security offered is perfectly sound. To provide adequate machinery for raising long-dated capital in amounts not sufficiently large for a public issue, i.e. amounts ranging from small sums up to say £200,000 or more, always presents difficulties. The expense of a public issue is too great in proportion to the capital raised, and therefore it is difficult to interest the ordinary investor; the Investment Trust Companies do not look with any great favour on small issues which would have no free market and would require closely watching; nor can any issuing house tie up its funds in long-dated capital issues of which it cannot dispose".[1]

In spite of wider investment by insurance companies and greater use of bank advances, this so-called "Macmillan" gap still appears to exist between the demand for and supply of intermediate long-period credit. The device of the Finance Corporation subsidized by the Bank of England, described earlier (p. 121) is, however, finding imitators arising in the market without any State subsidy. This sincere form of flattery may prove that provision of capital is a service necessary for the State to perform only as a priming operation—only to start the market mechanism moving. But it is doubtful whether the

[1]Cmd. 3897, pp. 173–4.

differential between the borrowing terms of small and large firms can ever be entirely closed, in view of the small firms' wider risk.[1]

§4 *Palliatives against the Hazards of Industry*

Money or "fiscal" compensation against the risks of life forms a large part of the policy of the "Welfare" State. It includes the system of Maternity Benefit, Family Allowances, Health Insurance, Pensions and Funeral Benefit, and National Assistance if benefits and allowances fail to meet the cost of subsistence—in fact compensating for hazards from the womb to the tomb. The avowed policy of "breaking up" the general Poor Law and dealing separately with the different causes of poverty (*see* p. 42-3) makes it fairly easy to distinguish the palliatives against the purely industrial hazards.

In the National Insurance Act of 1911 the principle was introduced of compulsory weekly contributions from employers and workers, and to a less extent the State, to cover most of the likely expenditure on benefits. The worker's contribution gave him a right to benefit without any question of a means test, and, to quote the words of Lord Beveridge, as he laboured on the scheme, "sets up the State as a comprehensive organism to which the individual belongs and in which he, under compulsion if need be, plays his part".[2] In the Act of 1911 unemployment was insured against in a few only of the more skilled trades, but the coverage was extended by the Act of 1920 to all manual employees and to non-manual employees earning less than £250 —subsequently raised to £420. In 1944 a special Ministry of National Insurance was formed to take over the all-in national insurance, including retirement pensions and insurance against injury as well as unemployment, advocated by the Beveridge Report of 1942, and carried into law by the Industrial Injuries Act and the National Insurance Act of 1946.

Both Acts left a considerable amount for the Ministry to deal with by regulations and set up independent Advisory Councils or Committees to advise the Minister on proposals for the regulations under the Act. All National Insurance

---

[1]*See* above p. 72
[2]Janet Beveridge, *Beveridge and His Plan*, 1954, p. 57.

regulations must be submitted in draft to the National Insurance Advisory Committee before being made or laid before Parliament. The committee is small and its members expert and independent. The procedure for making regulations under the Industrial Injuries Act is less formal, and membership of the Council is larger. Members are chosen not only for special technical knowledge, but as representatives of their organizations, thus conforming to the "demo-technocratic" pattern which so frequently surrounds modern State administration.

By the terms of the National Insurance Act the same benefits, based on subsistence, were to be paid to the industrially unemployed and retired as to the sick. Unemployment benefit was normally to last not more than thirty weeks, but "additional days" and extended benefit were payable to a worker with many years of contributions.

The State has long been concerned with industrial accidents (and occupational diseases) "arising out of, and in the course of employment", and has pursued a policy of prevention and cure. Greater safety and the prevention of accidents and diseases by coercive factory legislation has been discussed in Chapter III. This legislation, however, includes such curative rather than preventive measures as the provision of a first-aid box (and additional boxes for every hundred and fifty employed) with a responsible trained person in charge wherever more than fifty are employed. Before a complete cure of an injury can be effected, however, there will often be a period of incapacity and of absence from work with loss of wages. A responsibility for palliating or compensating the financial loss lies upon industry which has been met in three ways: (i) Employers' liability at common law (modified by various statutes) which was always part of the State's activity in keeping the ring round the industrial arena, but only arose if the employer could be proved negligent in his duties. "A master must use reasonable care in the choice of servants, must secure and maintain plant and appliances proper to the work in which they are to be used, and must finally combine personnel, plant and equipment in a safe system of working".[1] (ii) Workmen's compensation, which deems the employer to be an insurer of his employees. Under a series of

[1] W. Mansfield Cooper, *Outlines of Industrial Law*, 1954, p. 281.

Acts, beginning with that of 1897, this had been the chief statutory remedy for the injured worker until 1946. (iii) National Insurance similar to insurance against unemployment or sickness, introduced in the 1946 Industrial Injuries Act.

The Beveridge Report recommended a higher benefit for injury than for unemployment or sickness for three reasons : many industries vital to the community are also dangerous and the men who must enter them should have the assurance of special provision against risks; a man disabled during the course of his employment has been disabled while working under orders; only if special provision is made for the results of industrial accident and disease, irrespective of negligence, would it appear possible to limit the employer's liability at Common Law—a liability which has, however, by recent legislation and judgments in fact, greatly increased. Following Lord Beveridge's recommendation, while unemployment benefits (since July 1952) are for a single adult 32s. 6d. a week and for a couple 54s.; injury benefits are 55s. and 76s. 6d.

An accident may involve not, like unemployment, just a temporary absence from work, but a lifelong disablement or death. Disablement benefit will vary with the degree of disablement and the assessment is made by the medical boards and medical appeal tribunals according to what the claimant "has lost in health, strength and the power to enjoy life". Death benefit is paid to dependents weekly to avoid the mis-spending of a lump sum experienced in the past.

Insurance evens out income over time by paying individuals impoverished by some hazard out of a pool accumulated by contributions from all. It thus aims, as do so many other State activities, at greater equality of distribution and greater stability, or, from the individual's standpoint, greater security.

Insurance, however, can be, and is, undertaken by private organizations, and State action has had to be justified as an alternative or competitor to private enterprise. The most obvious justification occurs where, like unemployment, the hazards are too uncertain for private enterprise to cover. The application in 1911 of State insurance to unemployment was in fact a particularly bold adventure which private insurance companies had not attempted because of the difficulty of testing genuine involuntary unemployment. Any insurance of unemployment was indeed impossible without the service of State employment exchanges to help discover whether a worker was willing to accept work within his type of occupation; the initiation of State service and of State palliative were both in fact put forward by the same bold statesmen, Winston Churchill, then President of the Board of Trade, and William Beveridge, then a Civil Servant. Insurance against industrial disease is also difficult for private enterprise since it is the State itself that decides, on scientific grounds, when any particular disease can be described as occupational.

If insurance against unemployment and industrial diseases was a veritable void in the market mechanism of supply and demand, accident and retirement insurance showed gaps in the mechanism. Insurance companies are prepared to supply fiscal assurance against accident, retirement and death, for a premium; but only a certain proportion of workers have in fact so insured themselves, and the all-in insurance that is required can only be secured by coercion. Further, all-in compulsory insurance with contributions collected by weekly stamps bought in post offices is far cheaper in administrative cost than insurance with contributions collected competitively door to door—the doors for any one agent seldom being contiguous.

Recently a third alternative procedure has come to the fore to help the aim, at least, of a retirement pension—insurance, namely, neither by the individual concerned or by the State, but by the firm that employs him. This form of private but collective action has been stimulated by certain exemptions of the firm's contribution from State taxation and now covers a high proportion of all employees, particularly of the office staff, and the more permanent employees generally, of the larger firms. It may act as a supplement to State insurance, not however as a substitute. Without that insurance a totally uninsured gap would still be left among the less securely employed—precisely among those most likely to be in need of palliatives to provide a stable income.

The feeling of security which insurance should give against industrial hazards, must, however, depend mainly on the

E

comparison between a worker's income when employed and when unemployed, retired, injured or occupationally diseased. The unemployment benefits are at present very low in relation to earnings. The 32s. 6d. a week which an adult gets if single, and the 54s. if married, contrasts with men's all-industry average weekly earnings calculated in October 1953 as 189s. 2d. If unemployed a single man with average earning capacity would have lost at that date 83 per cent of his income, a married man 65 per cent. Benefits have since 1952 remained the same, but average money earnings continue to rise, so the disparity is widening. Clearly with these comparisons in mind a worker cannot feel very "secure" against redundancy. Though they just provide the recipient and his dependents with the bare necessaries of life, insurance benefits do not prevent his actual mode of living falling heavily below the standard to which his earnings have accustomed him. A direct aim of unemployment insurance is to compensate a worker for temporary redundancy due to a switch in demand or due to the reorganization or retooling of factories, and to stop him insisting on his right to a perpetual continuance of his old job, however unnecessary or out of date. Judging from the horror (and often strikes) against redundancy, this palliative, probably due to its quantitative inadequacy, does not seem to achieve its aim.

While the sufficiency of benefits to maintain life and efficiency breaks the vicious circle whereby unemployment breeds lower capacity to work and therefore further unemployment, unemployment benefits at the present level fail to give a sense of security. Possibly unemployment benefit should, like injury benefit, be differentiated above sickness benefit and retirement pensions—Lord Beveridge's argument for the higher injury benefit because some of the essential industries were particularly dangerous is equally applicable. Many essential industries, particularly the export industries with their uncertain markets, are particularly unemployment prone.

Beyond the question whether palliatives achieve their primary aim of giving security to the employee, lies the question whether they do not produce a "boomerang" repercussion by interfering with the aim of other State policies. Do retirement pensions, which are conditional on total earnings being no more than a low maximum (often only 50s. a week), not hasten retirement when national policy requires the employment of the largest possible man-power? Will not a high unemployment benefit encourage unemployment? Much depends on the "relativity" between the level of palliatives and of payments for work. During the depression of 1930-34 (when family allowances were paid to the unemployed but not to the employed) it was occasionally possible for a man with a large family to obtain more by unemployment benefit *plus* the children's allowance to the unemployed, than by wages *less* the expense of travelling and wearing presentable clothes. Now, with family allowance to parents whether they are unemployed or not, this financial incentive against work has ceased to operate—quite apart from the wide gap, already noted, between earnings and benefit.

CHAPTER VI

STATE OPERATION OF INDUSTRY

§1 *The Structure and Procedure of State Operation*

THE private operator or company displaced by the State did not operate an entire industry but only one firm or combine of firms within an industry. It is usually assumed, however, that substitution of State for private operation entails substitution of a complete monopoly for a number of firms in some degree of competition. All the Nationalization Acts of 1946-9 did in fact substitute State monopoly operation of whole industries for private competition or pseudo-competition within industries. This policy of granting the State a monopoly is, however, not the only alternative and in some industries the State is apparently found operating a firm in competition with other firms. Examples are Her Majesty's Stationery Office in the publishing industry, railway locomotive and wagon manufacture and repair, naval dockyards in the ship-building industry, arsenals and Royal Ordnance Factories in the ordnance and small arms and the explosives industry, government factories in the telegraph and telephone apparatus industry, and labour directly employed by local authorities in house-building. Competition is, however, more apparent than real, since the State is often operating in a separate section of the industry. Genuinely competing State-operated firms appear to be coming in road transport, and in industry have recently been advocated by one or two leaders of the Labour party for the special purpose of testing "as a yard-stick" the efficiency of the competing capitalist enterprise. In America this was one of the avowed aims of electrical power supply by the Tennessee Valley Authority.

Another existing form, alternative to the operation of a whole industry by the State authority is operation, either of the whole industry or of a firm within the industry, by a mixed State and private enterprise organization. An example is the Anglo-

Iranian Oil Company in which the British Government hold shares and the right to nominate directors. This "mixed" operation of industry, though frequent in Germany before 1914, is not widely practised or advocated today.

Whatever the existing or possible alternatives, many of them worth further attention, nationalization of industry in Britain today usually refers to monopoly operation of a whole industry by a purely State organization. Even within this limited definition a variety of forms of organization are possible, notably the ordinary form of a government department which was adopted for the business of the post office or, if a more independent authority was sought, a Board of representatives of the interests concerned on the model of Harbour or Water Boards. Neither of these forms was in fact adopted in 1946–49 by the Labour Government for a number of reasons, and a clear trend has set in towards one particular form, that of the Public Corporation.

The Public Corporation is known under different names for different industries, as the Coal Board, the Central Electricity Authority, the Gas Council, the Iron and Steel Corporation; but essentially the constitutions followed a similar pattern in each industry nationalized between 1946 and 1951.

On the economic and financial side the Corporation is planned to lead an independent life. To quote one of the constituting Acts, "revenues shall not be less than sufficient for meeting all outgoings properly chargeable to revenue account on an average of good and bad years". On the organizational and political side there is a complicated set of internal relationships between the Corporation and its central and regional Boards, managers, and officers, and externally an ambitious plan to bring in more external control such as that of Parliament and Consumers. The pattern of these internal and external relations as formally set up is best displayed by an organization chart.[1]

Above the Central Board of each Corporation with its subsidiary Boards in the line of command must be charted the appropriate Minister responsible to Parliament. For he appoints the members of the Board, and in the words of the 1946 Act setting up the Coal Board:

[1]Florence, *Logic of British and American Industry*, 1953, p. 241.

"(1) The Ministry may after consultation with the Board, give to the Board directions of a general character as to the exercise and performance of the Board of their functions in relation to matters appearing to the Minister to affect the national interest, and the Board shall give effect to any such directions. (2) In framing programmes of reorganization or development involving substantial outlay on capital account, the Board shall act on lines settled from time to time with the approval of the Minister. (3) In the exercise and performance of their functions as to training, education and research, the Board shall act on lines settled as aforesaid. (4) The Board must provide the Minister with information and facilities for the verification of information."

Where the Public Corporations differ one from another is mainly in degree of centralization and regionalization, depending largely on the technical characteristics of the industry. Electricity, for instance, can be switched from one region to another and there is a national grid. Gas on the other hand is less easily transmitted over distances. Consequently the regional or "Area" Gas Boards are more independent of the Gas Council than the regional Electricity Boards of the Electricity Authority. In fact, the Central Gas Council on which sit, under a chairman and deputy chairman, the chairmen of the Area Boards has only a few specified activities reserved to it. The Coal Board, which was the Public Corporation first constituted, was highly centralized

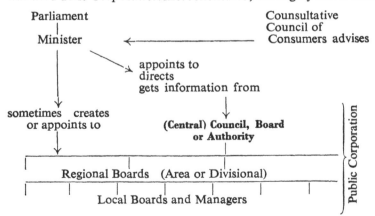

all embracing and managers have had to realize the importance of the joint consultative committees. But apart from the organization of the staff, no new pattern of industrial relations has been formed in the nationalized industries. The pattern already established in coal-mining and public utilities has simply been filled out and more uniformly applied; though not quite to the extent of making membership of Unions compulsory.[1]

So much has been written recently on the workers' position in industry that the consumers' interests have largely dropped out of sight. Judging from the writings of some social psychologists and industrial sociologists a reader would suppose that industry existed mainly not for producing goods, but for the sake of keeping up the morale of the workers and that problems of participation of workers in control of factory amenities and safety should take precedence over problems of low cost production and of low prices and efficient service to the consumer. This, the sociologists' order of precedence, is the reverse of the economists' and it is important to keep a balanced judgment. The relations of State-operated industry with the consumer are peculiar and must be analysed in some detail. The type of State-operation now under discussion involves monopoly over a whole industry. This gives wide play to the State operator; within the limits of covering costs imposed by the Nationalization Acts it is possible to charge prices to the consumer (like the flat postage rates for all distances) that will yield losses in certain lines, places or times, surpluses in others.

What the consumer expects from industry is a higher standard of living. In the public utilities and coal-mining so far nationalized, where the product is relatively uniform, this expectation is satisfied most simply and directly by a lowering of the prices of industrial products. Under nationalization, interest but no profit accrues to a special class, so that prices are related clearly to aggregate costs of production, and questions can be concentrated on the State's attention to reduction of costs. In coal-mining a merchant intervenes between producer and the domestic consumer, but in gas, electricity and industrial coal, State operation is solely responsible for prices to the consumer.

[1]Flanders, *Trade Unions*, Hutchinson's University Library, 1952, pp. 45–6.

As a matter of history the consumer has, since nationalization, suffered from repeated increases in the prices of the products (and services) of the nationalized industries, coal, gas and electricity among others, and has little chance of knowing whether the increases are justified, apart from a general inflation, on economic grounds. All that the consumers of national services and products see, is that rises in wages are continually being granted to the well-organized workers and prices raised to correspond, without much apparent effort to introduce special economies in the use of labour, and without much success in getting a higher productivity from labour to support the higher wages. Where nationalization has taken the place of municipal trading the consumer now has less knowledge and influence. His vote as a local citizen had in the past some effect on the policy of the municipal or borough council in keeping down prices. But once nationalized the issue of the prices charged by Public Corporations is submerged in country-wide election issues.

The consumer in a nationalized industry, like the worker, is not facing the private profit-makers and not liable to be exploited in the interest of maximum profit. But workers still exert pressure and perhaps increasing pressure, through their Trade Unions, even though industries are nationalized. This fact, added to the lack of competition, warrants an equivalent pressure from the consumer. He cannot turn from one competitor to another in search of lower prices, and unless aided by experts the consumer cannot judge how far he is being charged unnecessarily high. Three groups of experts are called for; the technologists, the production engineers and the economists.

Little argument is needed about the importance of the geologist, and the mining engineer in the coal industry, or the electrical and chemical engineer, in the electrical and gas industry. More argument perhaps is needed to convince the public of the importance of the time and motion, or work study, expert and of the production engineer; still more argument of the importance of the economist.

The economist and production engineer share an interest in the problems of the cost of supply. Here the coal industry differs radically from electrical and gas supplies in costs relative to total output. In the economists' phrase, mining is subject to the law of increasing cost, electrical and gas supply to the law of decreasing cost. While electricity and gas diminish in cost per unit the larger the scale of production; the extraction of coal increases in cost as more inaccessible places have usually to be tapped to find the additional coal. One factor of production, land and natural resources, is fixed and the amount of accessible coal of suitable qualities is limited. Manufacturing and, to a less extent, building follow, on the whole, the gas and electricity pattern of increasing return, since the element of fixed natural resources is small compared to the factors of labour, capital and management, expansible in the long run. The two sets of experts part company and political economists rather than production engineers are called for when consumers' demand, market considerations and the interests of the whole nation are involved.

The engineer may show that costs per unit would be very greatly reduced by producing more units of electricity on a larger scale with more powerful equipment, and this reduced cost would permit charging the consumer lower prices. But this statement, however expert, cannot be finally decisive for national policy. In the first place the consumer even at the lower prices will not demand or need an indefinitely increased supply. Both electricity and gas are, as the economist puts it, in joint demand with other commodities. They are used industrially to drive machines or actuate processes; they are used by the final consumer to light or heat spaces, or to cook food. The amount needed is therefore limited by the stock and calculable demand for, and supply of, machines, processes, space and food.

But there is a further set of considerations of special concern to the political element in political economy. Even if the low price of public utilities did stimulate increased consumption to carry off the increased production yielding lower costs, this increased consumption, because of the very cheapness of the product, may be wasteful; or increased production might be developed at the expense of other products. Developments in the equipment of electrical power stations might, for instance, prevent the resources required being used to supply machinery for other more urgent purposes; or building man-power might be switched to gasworks and power-stations from more necessary housing or factories. Before cost of supply considerations are allowed exclusively to determine price-policy, the consumers' demand curve must be estimated and also the distribution of national material and human resources. Ideally, the interests of consumers and citizens in general, present and future, must be taken into consideration, as well as the present consumers of one particular nationalized commodity.

With their wide possibilities of "play" in determining price levels and structures of prices the coal, gas and electricity authorities clearly have great responsibilities to consumers and the whole national economy. Some organ or organs are called for to advise the Public Corporation in fulfilling these responsibilities and also to balance the workers' organized pressures. Such organs have hitherto taken the form of occasional departmental or *ad hoc* committees with a duty to report, and of permanent consumers' consultative councils as well as Parliamentary supervision "built in" (as the Chart on page 134 shows) to the general nationalized organization.

In July 1951, a Departmental Committee was appointed by the Minister of Fuel and Power, with Viscount Ridley in the chair, to report on "the best use of our fuel and power resources, having regard to present and prospective requirements and in the light of technical developments". The Committee took their terms of reference "as covering all use of fuel and power resources, both by the ultimate consumers—householders, manufacturers, traders and others—and by the industries which convert primary fuels (chiefly coal and oil) into secondary forms (mainly gas, coke and electricity); . . . (and it) studied how, on what scale, and in what patterns the different consumers use and may in future use fuel and power".[1]

Price policy on which scale and pattern of consumption so much depend, was reported upon separately for coal and for electricity and gas. On the price level for coal the committee split exactly equally in number—and perhaps weight! Four, including the two professors—one an economist—advocated a steep rise in prices; four, including the chairman, little change.

[1] Report of the Committee on *National Policy for the Use of Fuel and Power Resources*, 1952, p. iii. Cmd. 8646.

The main reason for advocating a rise in the price levels is significant of the thinking of economists both on possible maldistribution and possible waste of resources, when a product is raised under conditions of increasing cost.

". . . in comparing the value of resources used in one industry with the value of the same resources to some other industry, it is necessary to think only in terms of the little more or the little less. The practical problem is whether some part of the resources should be shifted from one industry to another, and the value of this marginal part only is relevant; the price of coal should correspond not to the average cost of producing all the coal mined, but to the cost of producing additional supplies. The demarcation of marginal output is in practice somewhat arbitrary: a smaller or larger tonnage might be taken. We have been told by the National Coal Board that 7 million tons of their annual output is produced at a loss of fifteen shillings or more a ton. For practical purposes this may be taken as the relevant marginal output; since at present the coal price level is based on average cost, the marginal cost on this interpretation is at least fifteen shillings higher. Hence, these members conclude that the present price of coal in this country is in general *at least* fifteen shillings a ton too low."[1]

The "overriding principle" given by the other half of the committee for maintaining the present price policy based on average, not marginal costs, was that:

"Coal is so important to the economy that it should be sold at the lowest price which is consistent with the National Coal Board's covering its costs. Indeed they assume that one advantage of the nationalization of coal is to realize this principle, and that to charge coal consumers £200 million more than the total cost of production would be quite unjustifiable."[1]

Both halves of the committee agreed that prices were important in checking the waste of coal "both by discouraging people from using coal for inferior purposes (e.g. as ballast) and by stimulating users to burn coal efficiently". Avoidance of waste of coal is, to crown all, important because wasteful use in open fires means smoke and air pollution. In fact, prices of coal

[1]*Op. cit.* pp. 15–16 and 17.

were increased in July 1951, according to quality and use from 9*s.* to 19*s.* a ton.

Electricity and gas, produced under conditions of decreasing costs, do not give rise to such diametrically opposed policies for this relation of the price level to costs. But industrial policy cannot decide on prices in isolation from output and there remains the question of the output to aim for. In the basic industries which have been the first to be nationalized, price is largely subsidiary to output policy and in their activity of planning investment and man-power mobilization Public Corporations have set themselves output targets. In 1949 the Coal Board, for instance, published a *Plan for Coal* aiming at 240 million tons of coal being mined and sold in 1961–65. Since 1949 there has been a spate of revisions of this output target; the Ridley Committee upward, many economists downward.

The contending arguments are based on the possibilities of any considerable substitution for, or economy in, coal. Shall the consumer be free to burn as much coal, gas or electricity as he wants according to his demand at the prices which costs allow; or shall the consumer be "guided" by prices into using what is "best" for his own or for society's needs? A "need" I define as "any thing or service the consumer *ought* to have, to keep alive, and healthy, or to keep efficient, or simply because somebody (not necessarily himself) thinks he ought to have it"[1]—often for reasons of public health. The average English consumer wants open fires which are wasteful of coal and pollute the air. Gas or smokeless fuel fires or else central heating, engineers tell us, are the most economical for space warming. Should not State-operated monopolies, who have it in their power, so co-ordinate their prices that the consumer is given an incentive to use more gas or central heating, and to use less electricity or raw coal?

Most English economists today, like the Ridley Committee, seem to favour technical efficiency and satisfaction of needs rather than wants and are even prepared for the State to subsidize technically efficient heating apparatus.[2] They see little aim,

---

[1]*Logic of British and American Industry*, 1953, p. 98. Since welfare as now used appears to muddle wants and needs, I avoid using that word.

[2]e.g., I. M. D. Little, *The Price of Fuel*, 1953, p. 121.

otherwise, in nationalizing basic industries. But it must be realized that this policy is one of consumption planning, not responding freely to the consumer's demands; forswearing in fact his sovereignty; and that preferring the one policy to the other is a value-judgment.

Apart from the effect upon amount in use of the *level* of prices, coal, gas and electricity each, according to their technical characteristics, present special problems in the *structure* of prices. The Public Corporation first had to replace the bewildering variety of tariffs and accounting methods (as also technical equipment) to which they succeeded, by certain standard practices and specifications.

Under State monopolies it would be possible to go further and to let price structure ignore cost differentials so long as total sales did not fall short of total costs. Thus, uniform prices might be charged in all areas, rural or urban, regardless of the economies of population density. But the Ridley Committee recommended, on the whole, charging strictly according to cost of supply and paying attention to technical cost characteristics. Electricity cannot, like gas, be stored, so the electricity tariff should discourage, by a high price, consumption of electricity during peak hours. Gas is locally produced, its works vary more widely in size than electricity stations and cost tends to vary accordingly. So the prices charged by the Gas Boards should, according to the committee, reflect local differences in costs of supply.[1] Coal is costly to transport and is produced (of varying heat content, size and preparedness) in widely scattered coalfields. The Ridley Committee recommended "a standard system of coal specification and classification to enable the consumer to select whatever coal he judges best . . . for his particular use". "The price structure for coal should embody sufficient flexibility to enable prices for each type of coal to equate demand with available supply in each consumption area."[2]

To sum up. Under a State-operated monopoly there is the possibility of a wide variety of price policies, favourable or unfavourable to the consumer. The workers have successfully pressed for higher wages, with or without promising, or achieving,

[1]*op. cit.* p. 63.
[2]*op. cit.* p. 57.

E*

higher productivity, and in the absence of cost reduction higher prices have been the consequence. Economists, in the long-term national interest, have pressed against waste and maldistribution of national resources and, through their membership of official *ad hoc* committees have for these reasons often urged higher prices. Higher prices may however cloak unnecessarily high costs of production and distribution and inefficient production engineering and management. Should the consumers as well as national interests, not, therefore, have some formal and continuous recognition in the State organization of monopolies?

§3 *The Formal Embodiment of Consumer and National Interests*

Of the several directions of possible pressure, workers' pressure has, under nationalization, proved much the strongest organized. Trade Unions have taken up the specific grievances of members, often a matter of the interpretation of rules, first at factory, pit or station level, then local, then district, and then national level; they are also organized to participate in wide-reaching decision about wages, hours and other working conditions. Should consumers not have some similar organization both for considering individual grievances, and for discussing general policies affecting their interest before policies are officially promulgated and for reviewing them when their effects are seen? In short, should consumers not have the same semi-judicial and pre- and post-legislative activities granted them, as the workers' Trade Unions take up as a matter of course? Trade Unions have their own paid officials independent of the nationalized industries to support the grievances they consider justified and to work up general demands, and recently have developed research departments.

In the Acts setting up State operation, Consumers' 'Consultative' Councils were formally built into the structure: two for coal mining, Industrial and Domestic, at the discretion of the Minister; one in every region obligatory for gas and electricity, with a plan for bodies still more local. All members of these Councils are appointed and dismissable by the Minister, and most now actually appointed are lay rather than expert; members on the Gas and Electricity Councils are often elected councillors of the local authorities in the region. The Herbert

Committee recommended, however, that these councillors should be fewer, and of the same ability as required of other members.[1] The Councils' chairmen are by statute members of the Area Board, making and reviewing policy; and in reviewing on their own initiative or interpreting the policy in individual cases, the Consumers' Councils were all given some share.

In the procedure laid down for the Consumers' Councils the trend shown in the Gas and Electricity Acts, passed later than the Coal Act, is for considerable legislative and semi-judicial powers to be assigned. In order of stages in government procedure the Area Consumers' Councils have:

1. Opportunity to comment on proposals of the Boards before a decision is reached.

2. Right to consider and make recommendations to be notified to the Board on any matter relating to product, service, or facilities on their own initiative or upon representation from a (presumably aggrieved) consumer.

3. Right of appeal to the central authority (for Electricity) or the Minister (for Gas) on any matter notified to the Boards without avail.

Experience since the date of nationalization is that these councils, or at least their chairmen, have been fairly successful in coping with individual grievances about price, quality, service and even high-hatting by officials. They have had injustices remedied in the interpretation of the rules. In the making or reviewing of rules and general policy Consumers' Councils have been unable, however, to stand up to the Boards, partly because their constituents (unless industrial consumers, who hardly need their help) are unorganized, partly because they are not independent and cannot command from the Boards the data they require, and partly because something more than a small office staff is necessary. In the author's own experience the Boards are quite as unwilling to have their work independently investigated and ventilated as most private businesses and since they hold a monopoly this resentment of inquiry closes the window finally on the whole industry. If policies are to be constructively reviewed, with alternative policies suggested, the Consumers' Councils need an effective staff to conduct independent inquiries

[1] *op. cit.* pp. 149–50.

into policy matters. What staff exists at present is mostly part
and parcel of the Board's organization.

It would be far too costly in expert man-power to have such
a separate research staff for each Consumer Council, but a central
research organization, independent of the Public Corporation
management, might be organized to serve all Consumers' Councils. Alternatively, or in addition, investigations might be undertaken under contract by the universities or independent research
organizations.

Our discussion of pressures upon the Public Corporations of
State-operated industries has made one thing clear. A further
interest has to be represented in nationalized undertakings—
the nation as a whole and as a continuing entity. Even if present-
day workers and consumers were individually satisfied, the
question would still remain whether national resources were not
being wasted and maldistributed by prices not adjusted to long-
term costs. This third, national, interest and the need for the
co-ordination of all interests is admitted by the public obligations
imposed in the Corporations' originating statute, and by the
overriding authority given in the structure and procedure of
State operation to the appropriate Ministry, and its responsibility
to Parliament.

Public Corporations consisting of the central and regional
Boards and their officials, have been substituted for the capitalist
sole traders, partnerships or companies and, in the main, appear
to act more or less similarly towards workers and towards
consumers. They expect to charge the consumer prices that will
avoid a loss when, among other costs, wage rates agreed with
Trade Unions have been paid to employees. As well as the
obligation to be a model employer in protecting the workers
from exploitation by participating *with* him to the utmost possible,
other obligations imposed by the State on private enterprise
remain, such as submission to controls over prices and quantities,
or giving information. But the Public Corporations are using
public money like any Department of State; so further, strict,
bureaucratic obligations are imposed such as accounting returns,
not to mention a certain glare of publicity and press search-
lights peering for cases of mismanagement. Enterprising management which must take risks—nothing venture, nothing gain—is

made more difficult, yet it is recognized that industries once they are State-operated must have a closer relation with the State government than a mere substitution of Public Corporation for capitalist enterprise in the general social structure. The State operation of an industry thus involves a complex constitution in which the State government formally takes its share in ruling with the Public Corporation itself, with the workers and with the consumers.

The present rule-share of the State government consists on paper (by virtue of the statutes) in the appropriate Ministry's power of appointing members of the Boards; or giving the Board, after consultation with it, directions of a general character on matters affecting the national interest; and of getting information from this (Central) Board. The Minister's share is particularly stressed in matters of reorganization, capital development, training, education and research.

Since the paper constitution was written, the Minister's powers have increased beyond what was probably contemplated, particularly in the matter of wage-policy. This *de facto* deviation beyond the *de jure* powers was largely the result of the continued inflation in price and costs of living, stimulating Trade Unions continually to call for increases in money wages that the Corporations were unwilling to grant, at least without continuous increases in prices. Disputes and indeed regular rows developed in consequence, in which the Minister was called to adjudicate, not only because of the days lost in strikes but because of the risk of repercussions upsetting established differential wage-rates.

The Minister has acquired power also because he is a member of a Cabinet that has an all-round supervision over the nation's affairs. Inflation raised problems for the whole economy and in any case the policy of one industry has to be co-ordinated with that of the others. General directions allowed the Ministry on matters of national interest are particularly relevant to this co-ordination, and "general" is an elastic term!

Parliament, moreover, became involved in most of the rows. Under the paper, statutory, constitution Parliament's share in the control of State-operated industries was mainly confined to calling for papers and otherwise obtaining information by means of the annual reports and accounts of the Corporation, or to questions to Ministers, or to debates on various motions, in committee of supply or on Bills dealing with the relevant industries. Feeling has developed in Parliament however and has been expressed by a Select Committee of the House of Commons, sitting in 1953, that the Public Corporations should be made more regularly accountable to the nation.

"The need for accountability in the Nationalized Industries arises from the vast amount of capital, and of income and expenditure involved in concerns which are under public ownership; the charges upon consumers and users of the necessities of civilized life which they provide; and the Treasury guarantee of the interest paid on the stock issued in respect of the various Nationalized Industries."[1]

Accordingly the Select Committee recommended a Standing Committee of the House with an experienced professional staff to obtain information beyond that published in each industry's reports and accounts.

The main argument against such a Standing Committee was that it would impede the working of the Nationalized Industries and destroy initiative in them. Much questioning, which the Central Board must meet, might indeed reverse the trend towards decentralization. Mr. Herbert Morrison thought it might "unnerve" the ordinary business men who are running, in the main, the publicly owned industries and might tend to develop in them a rather red-tapish, unadventurous and conventionally Civil Service frame of mind. He pointed out that "Parliament did deliberately decide in place of a State Department, with all the consequences of a State Department including Select committees on accounts and so on, to set up public corporations and to leave them a good deal of freedom".[2] Nevertheless the arguments for such a Standing Committee, mainly perhaps the need of accountability for the spending of the taxpayers' money, won the day. If created it was hoped the committee would conduct itself so as to be "regarded by the Board not as an enemy, or a critic, but as a confidant, and a protection against irresponsible pressure, as well as a guardian of the public interest".[3]

[1]Report from the Select Committee on *Nationalized Industries*, House of Commons, July 23, 1953, p. iv.
[2]*op. cit.* p. 56.
[3]*op. cit.* p. vii.

Some industries deserve more Parliamentary attention than others, particularly industries where subsidies may have to be paid or much capital borrowed, or where important consequences beyond the industry itself may follow from its policies. But in all industries likely to be nationalized there is always some degree of responsibility (over and above that to the workers and the consumers) both to Parliament, as keeper of the Nation's purse, and to the wider public of the nation as a whole, for whom reports are published and a general duty of service is owed. The Public Corporation has, in short, to be judged in the light of labour, consumer, financial and public relations.

The upshot of this discussion into possible structures embodying special interests and general national considerations, is agreement that the State operation of industry must be inquired into from time to time, both to test the efficiency of past performance and to lay the foundation for new plans and policies. The inquiry should be thorough, with expert staff on a fairly large scale; but should not be so frequent as continually to be badgering those managing the Public Corporations. The main difficulty is the auspices under which the inquiry should be organized. It must be independent, and therefore not under the auspices of the Corporations themselves; and the necessary thoroughness and large scale of the inquiry precludes the consumers of single industries instituting separate projects of research. In any case, the policies of one industry affect the interests of others so that inquiries should not be viewed only from the angle of the single industry. Possibly a link could be forged between the Consumers' Councils and some research and efficiency unit. The unit's governing body might contain representatives not only of the Corporation of each nationalized industry likely to use its services, but a representative of the industry's Consumers' Councils.

§4 *The Aims and Limits of State Operation*

The laws nationalizing various industries followed upon considerable agitation. For many years before the Acts of 1946–49, Trade Union Congresses and Conferences of the Labour Party had been passing resolutions in favour of nationalizing industry. The very constitution of the Labour party, drawn up in 1918, states as one chief object:

> "To secure for the producers by hand or by brain, the full fruits of their industry and the most equitable distribution thereof that may be possible on the basis of the common ownership of the means of production."

After 1918, as political power approached, the policy of the party became more specifically one of nationalizing stated industries. The preambles and speeches accompanying conference resolutions set forth the aims to be achieved, gave "reasons" for selecting one industry rather than another—and public opinion has to some extent concurred with some of the selections, at least as a justified deviation from *laissez-faire*.

Outside manufacturing and mining, some economic activities, it is agreed, must be performed gratis or at a loss, either (like education, health measures or building houses and housing estates) for some highly valued common good; or like road-making and maintenance, because collecting the price from users is administratively too costly. These loss-making activities will not be undertaken by private enterprise, and once the decision is taken to charge below cost or not charge at all, then, apart from charity or State subsidies, State-operation follows of necessity.

Where, on the trading principle, however, prices to cover costs are to be charged, special reasons are usually advanced for the deviation from *laissez-faire* which substitutes the State for the private trader. The main reasons for the wide adoption of this policy in Britain by the Labour Government of 1945–50 were clearly put forward by the Labour Party itself in three paragraphs of their *Labour and the New Society* issued in 1950.

(*i*) "Public ownership is a means of ensuring that monopolies do not exploit the public. Private monopolists have too much power over the happiness and destinies of their fellow men. Where monopoly is inevitable there should be public ownership."

Two aims are here involved, no exploitation of the demands of the consumer for the private profit of a few persons, and greater equality and democratic dispersion of power between persons. Public opinion today supports, on the whole, these economic and political aims, but whether nationalization is the most effective means to achieve them remains an open question. The State, as already shown, has adopted alternative means of curbing monopoly, and progressive taxation has succeeded in considerably modifying the inequality of incomes.

(ii) "Public ownership is a means for controlling the basic industries and services on which the economic life and welfare of the community depend. Control cannot be safely left in the hands of groups of private owners not answerable to the community."

The aims involved in this paragraph are connected with the economy as a whole rather than with the relations of individual persons. The adjective "basic" which has already appeared in our discussion, refers to the power of certain industries to affect the economy as a whole more than other industries. To achieve the aim of progress in standards of living with stability and full employment which "welfare of the community" connotes, control over policy in providing iron and steel or living needs is obviously more important than providing luxuries.

(iii) "Public ownership is a way of dealing with industries in which inefficiency persists and where the private owners lack either the will or the capacity to make improvements."

This paragraph involves questions of business rather than philosophy, means rather than aims; it may put limits on the extension of State operation if nationalization is shown not to be efficient, when applied to industries with certain technical and economic characteristics.

The need for public control of "basic" industries and services and the existence of private inefficiency can be split up further. Basic industries may be taken certainly to denote industries whose policy may fundamentally affect general stability and progress; and possibly to include industries, like gas or water supply, in common consumption. Inefficiency again, as the quotation suggests, may be due to two causes; lack of will or lack of capacity. For instance, the private firm may lack the will or capacity to grow larger or to invest in capital equipment or to employ scientific experts, though all these factors—larger size, more intense capitalization and application of research— are necessary to the efficiency of that industry.

Whether or no its will to invest is as strong as efficiency demands, the nationalized sector of industry, particularly electricity supply, has taken up a very high proportion of the total national capital formation of the post-war years. In the three years 1951 to 1953 the Public Corporations, including Iron and Steel, operated no more than 20 per cent of the national economy. But they spent £665 millions on plant and machinery —over half of the £1,294 millions similarly spent by persons and companies combined. By this large investment, nationalized industries go some way towards achieving the aim, cited earlier, of indirectly controlling "the economic life of the community" and affecting general progress beyond the limits of the industrial sector. In fact, the great investment of electricity, coal (and iron and steel) can well justify their nationalization as steps to total national planning if such planning is wanted. But it does not follow that nationalization increases efficiency by enhancing the willingness of labour or of management. Labour, in mines as in railways has not by its record of strikes or threats of strikes shown much variation in attitude, nor do the usual tests of efficiency, such as labour turnover, absenteeism, productivity per man show, in the industries nationalized, much change either absolutely, or relatively to the "control group" of industries remaining in private hands. In the iron and steel industry which will be discussed later, production, total and per man, has increased steadily whether nationalized or not. But in the coal industry comparing 1951–53 with 1938, before nationalization, total output has fallen slightly, productivity per manshift increased slightly from 1·14 to 1·20 tons, less than the rate of mechanization would have pre-supposed; while overall absence rates increased from 6·44 to 12·22 per cent. Management efficiency is less easy to test. If the orthodox test of profits or surplus be applied, coal, though not gas or electricity, comes out badly. While recording "moderate surpluses since vesting day", the Herbert Committee on the Electricity Industry considers that "the Authority's passive attitude towards redundancy has led to a disinclination of management at all levels to seek out under-employment".[1]

One or two further grounds underlie State operation of industries, though less explicitly stated as "reasons". One is the need to conserve for future generations resources such as forests and minerals which private enterprise might exploit for immediate profit. Another is close integration with existing national activities, such as defence.

How far do these reasons, grounds and aims for State operation apply in all industries already nationalized? And can they be shown to apply at all to other industries, thus constituting a possible case for further nationalization? In 1953 I put forward a list of characteristics, relevant to nationalization, denoted for brevity by capital letters, "so arranged that those occurring earlier in the alphabet refer to characters of demand for the industry's products and services, and letters occurring later in the alphabet refer to characters of supply. M and Q, in the middle of the alphabet, denoting the need and fact of monopoly and need and lack of capital equipment, are due to both demand and supply conditions."[2] These characteristics are not necessarily of equal importance, but are worth listing as possible hypotheses to explain why certain industries are nationalized and others in the arena of controversy.

CHARACTERISTICS RELEVANT TO NATIONALIZATION

Demand Conditions

 B—Basic to the industrial economy, mainly early-stage producer's (capital) goods or services to production

 C—Common service to the community—goods and services demanded by the bulk of consumers

 E—Education need

 F—Conservation for possible future demand

 G—Other reasons for Gratis provision (not E or H)

 H—Health need

Demand and Supply Conditions

 M—Need, likelihood or fact of Monopoly

 Q—Need (and lack) of large Capital Equipment

[1]*op. cit.*, p. 145.
[2]Florence, *Logic of British and American Industry*, 1953, p. 227.

Supply Conditions

   R—Technical and market conditions allow routine management
   S —Large sized plants or firms typical
   X—Need for (scientific) experts
   Y—Integrated with existing State activities because of technical
        linkage; e.g. Arsenals with Defence
   Z—Organization previous to Nationalization inefficient or high
     in cost

Table 6 adds to the industries already nationalized, or, like road making and maintenance always State operated, some industries proposed for further nationalization by representative organizations such as the Labour Party or the Trade Union Congress, and it is important to consider how far the relevant characteristics (denoted by letters) apply to these industries proposed for nationalization as well as to those already nationalized.

A high proportion of possible letters can probably be bestowed upon coal-mining and the public utilities—gas, electricity; and also upon road-making. Coal, electricity and roads are (B) basic to the economy and, as well as gas, are (C) in common use. There are practical reasons such as the difficulty of collecting tolls, why roads are (G) free of charge (i.e. "gratis"). All except coal must, for efficient operation, be (M) monopolies, and all except perhaps roads make use of (Q) costly equipment. Their management, on the whole, is mainly (R) routine and calls for (X) scientific "expertize" rather than enterprise and (with the exception of minor roads built and maintained locally) large size (S) units are probably more economical and efficient in these industries than small. These relevant technical and economic characteristics on the demand and supply side are not lightly attributed to the different industries, but require careful consideration, measurement and tests. Following the precedent of the inquiries made before introducing factory legislation and other policies on behalf of second or third parties, the State also made inquiries before taking over the operation of industries as a first party "on its own".[1]

How far are these characteristics valid for the industries proposed to be, but not yet, nationalized—industries in the very

[1]*See* Florence *op. cit.* p. 233–4

TABLE 6: INDUSTRIES ALREADY NATIONALIZED OR PROPOSED FOR NATIONALIZATION AND THEIR RELEVANT CHARACTERISTICS

Industry	History and Description	Relevant Economic and Technical Characteristics
COAL MINING .	Nationalization Act, 1947	B C F Q R S X Z
MANUFACTURING: Iron and Steel .	Nationalization Act, 1949. (Iron and Steel Corporation). Denationalization Act, 1953	B Q R S X y[1]
Basic Chemicals Sugar Cement Machine Tools	Proposed for Nationalization by Labour Party 1947–55	B M Q S X C M Q R S B M Q R S B C r y
Oil Refining . .	Some mixed firms with State appointed directors	M Y[2]
Publishing · .	H.M. Stationery Office. Competitive	E R X Y
Armaments . .	Dockyards, Arsenals, Royal Ordnance Factories. Competitive	X Y
PUBLIC UTILITIES: Gas . . . Electricity . . Water . . . Roads . .	Nationalization Act, 1948 Nationalization Act, 1947 Mainly local authority Local Authorities subsidized by State. Building through private contractor; maintenance by direct labour	C M Q R S X Z B C M Q R S X C M R X B C G M R X
BUILDING: Government Offices	Office of Works	Y
Houses to let Schools	Local Authorities (subsidized by State) through private contractor, or direct labour	CH EY

[1]See p. 158.
[2]Use by Navy.

arena of controversy? The most heavily fought of all controversies is that over the earlier processes of the Iron and Steel industry. These processes, nationalized once, then denationalized and then proposed for renationalization in the Labour Party programme for the 1955 election, include iron-smelting, conversion of iron to steel and steel rolling mills. They require large and highly equipped plants and fairly routine management with an expert rather than "enterprise" outlook, compared to the later processes manufacturing a wide variety of products for a multiplicity of markets. Their product is basic to the whole economy, since fixed capital investment in other industries is largely made of iron and steel. The industry is involved in all plans for re-equipment.

The earlier processes of the iron and steel industry thus merit the letters B Q R S X. On the other hand, it may often be uneconomic to separate control of the earlier from the later less routine, less basic, processes which stay under capitalist control; the letter Y standing for integration with linked State activities must not only be refused to Iron and Steel as a point in favour of nationalization, but a small y may be written in to mark a point against nationalization, as bringing about disintegration from linked capitalist activities.

Except for the unemployment of men and of physical capacity from 1929 to 1934—an important enough exception—it is not easy to make out the case that in recent years the management and government of the British iron and steel industry has been particularly inefficient either on the technical, the economic or the labour relations aspects. Output per worker has, since 1937, increased as fast as the average of British industries, and total output faster up to 1954, than in most other West European countries. Moreover, to quote Knowles, "for some time the iron and steel industry has been reported the brightest spot in the country's industrial relations; indeed, apart from the industry's participation in the General Strike, there has not been a widespread strike for half a century".[1] Where capitalist steel making was mainly deficient was in its long-term plans for capital investment; the national economy suffers today from shortage of efficiently produced steel. It is not sure,

[1] *Strikes*, p. 172.

however, that the usual directive set a nationalized corporation to make revenue meet outgoings would have remedied the deficiency.

In the official Labour Party programme for the 1955 election campaign, branches of two manufacturing industries not hitherto nationalized at all were proposed for the public sector; machine tools and chemicals; and, in earlier programmes two other industries, sugar and cement. No official inquiry, preceded the proposal for these industries, but pertinent information is offered by the census of production.

The cement industry and the earlier processes in chemicals can be classed as basic, sugar as in common use, all three industries have large plants prevailing, a structure favourable to monopoly, and a need for high capital equipment. The cement and sugar industries each make one fairly homogeneous group of products and are comparatively routine to that extent. They are not linked with State activities but are differentiated from other industries and therefore easy to operate under one authority without leaving the State competitive fringes. In neither industry have the leading firms been accused of inefficiency. No large Y and no Z can therefore be allocated.

Letters are not so clearly allocated to the machine-tool industry, however. Characteristics of the industry include common use, in the sense that nearly every industry nowadays uses machines, and that the metal-working industries use machines no less universally than others—the machines in their case being called machine-tools. As well as in common use, the machine-tool industry can also perhaps be characterized as basic, since the machines it makes include machines to make machines and much of the "investment" activity, on which economists today put such stress, involves equipment with new machines. The capacity of the industry might limit the expansion of the whole economy and, on the other hand, the slightest let-up in economic activity might, by the process of deceleration after acceleration, throw machine-makers into idleness. Though "common" and "basic", it is doubtful, however, whether the machine-tool industry has a sufficiently routine nature, whether unusually large-sized plants and other monopoly conditions prevail, and whether the industry does need a particularly large capital equipment or does not integrate (or get integrated by) other capitalist industries too far.[1]

§5 *The State as Consumer and Trader in Industry*

The possible limits of State operation, and the question as to which particular industries may fall inside or outside these limits, cannot be settled without taking into consideration the wide variety of industries at each stage of the whole productive process. Industries produce goods out of raw materials for consumers in a market. These consumers may be producers at the next state in the manufacturing process, or may be traders distributing the goods, or may be the final consumers. The State itself is found among all three consumer types. To illustrate from one line of production, the State is a consumer of coal for gas production, trades in (i.e. buys and sells) heating apparatus for burning gas, and in its administrative offices finally consumes the gas itself. Illustrating more widely, the State buys raw materials for production by its nationalized industries, has traded in commodities (e.g. between 1947 and 1954 bought from and sold to private industry through the Raw Cotton Commission) and "finally" consumes munitions of war. Industry, as defined in this book, is not directly concerned with trading or final consumption. But the fact that the State is a buyer and seller and, still more important, that it is a buyer for further production or for distribution, strongly affects the scope of its industrial operations. The economy of integrating technically linked production has already been given as a reason (the "Y" condition) for the State operation of certain industries linked with other State activities. The State prints, makes transport and telephone equipment and armaments, and maintains an Office of Works, because it distributes printed reports, operates transport and communications, uses weapons and requires buildings, and thus a market is assured without requiring great enterprise.

Equally important as a large source of State consumption are the free, "gratis" provisions by the central or local government

[1]Detailed statistical evidence for or against nationalization of these six or seven manufacturing industries in the arena of controversy is given in Florence *Present Problems in the Nationalization of British Industries*, Indian Journal of Economics, July 1955, pp. 41-6.

for the sake of general health and education and amenity, or for administrative convenience, notably the provision of schools, housing and trading estates, whole New Towns, and the construction and maintenance of roads.

Like the aims involved, the relation of the State to final consumption may be various. The local authority itself is the final user of schools; lets houses to private familes at a low rent subsidized by the State; but charges nothing for the use of roads. Yet, though trading relations with the consumer are different, the relations involved between the State and the industrial producer are much the same; the State, either the Central Government, or the Local Authority, usually puts the work out to contract and the role of the State is like that of a private trader or consumer, except that special provisions may be inserted in the contract. The most famous special provision is the Fair Wages Clause, but provisions may refer to the condition of the work as well as working conditions. Thus houses on estates, contracted for by municipalities, are usually laid out and designed with more consideration for social amenities and simplicity of architecture than the private speculative builders' houses, sold to the private consumer, so often jerry-built, gothic-featured, ribbon-developed. Again, the contractor building roads can be held to certain specifications aiming at greater safety and even to more pleasant "landscaping". Though not the actual operator of the industry, the State as a buyer for direct consumption or further trading can thus influence the operator towards certain aims valued by public opinion.

State consumption and trading in free or subsidized, as in other goods, may however always extend into State operation. Some local authorities, considering building contractors' operations too expensive, may try to operate themselves, employing building labour "direct"; and road maintenance and improvement as distinct from road construction is, in fact, usually operated direct.

§6 A Summary

(1) Traditional forms carry great weight in Britain, and the shape that the structure and procedure of nationalized industries is taking proves no exception. The traditional forms are that of

the joint stock company in the actual operation of an industry, with interference by a complex of controls, participations, safeguards, services, inquiries and palliatives, provided by departments of State, by Trade Unions or by special bodies partly representing both or appointed by the State as representing independent and expert opinion.

Essentially, this traditional pattern has not changed with the substitution of the Public Corporation for private enterprise in the operation of industries. Whatever novelties may have been envisaged the new institutions have tended to fall into the accustomed groove. This may not be just a sociological stereo-typing, but the rational consequence of organizing for technical and economic efficiency, common to all large-scale business today.

(2) The repetition of the traditional patterns extends from its external relations to the internal organization of the Public Corporation. According to the British Constitution, top Government is embodied in a committee called the Cabinet. Similarly top-management of each Nationalized industry is embodied in a committee usually called a Board. The Boards of the Public Corporations are, with their various types of member, formed, sometimes deliberately formed, on the model of the Board of Directors of Companies. With the enormous size of the national undertakings, problems of decentralization are tackled on the lines of those larger Joint Stock Companies who own, or hold the shares of, many subsidiary plants. More important than ever is the practice, developed by large companies, of carefully defining the powers to be centrally reserved and carefully controlling delegated powers. With structures and procedure similar to that of the large-scale private enterprise and a partly similar minimum duty not to make a long-term financial loss, the Public Corporation is, perhaps naturally inclined to adopt similar policies and to fall into the routine of the market economy.

(3) The process of nationalization has in Britain been piecemeal, industry by industry; but once an industry is taken over, it is taken over as a whole. This is something new and is an attempt to create a new structural level between the authority of the State and the hitherto topmost operating authority in the market, namely

the firm or combine. This structure operating a whole industry forms, side by side with Trade Unions, Employers' Associations, Trade Associations, Industrial Development Councils, and so on, one of the "collectives" on which modern British political philosophy relies so much in reality. In spite of repeated assertions of the "end of *laissez-faire*", Britain has emphatically not substituted State planning for a *laissez-faire* where the State "keeps the ring" and only interferes when a case can be made out. Instead, the country has developed something much more original, indeed almost aboriginal: the doctrine, or rather the practice of *laissez collectives faire*. It is not yet a doctrine and, being English, may never become a doctrine. But it is in wide operation. Wage-policy is not planned nationally but, subject to minimum wages in unorganized industries, is left to Employers' Associations and Trade Unions to fight out, industry by industry, through collective bargaining; the State merely keeping the ring to see fair play without too many, or too protracted, stoppages of work. Thus the Public Corporation is left to fight out its price and output policies against pressure from the workers already well organized, and from consumers whom the State itself strives to organize.

(4) From one aspect, the State, in its essential capacity, still only keeps the ring round the collective bargaining and higgling of the Corporation with the pressure groups. From another aspect, the Public Corporation procedure represents an orderly devolution of State power to the whole-of-an-industry level; and through this procedure some effects are visible of a striving towards aims beyond that of an individualistic market economy. Within the limits of an industry's technical and economic suitability for State operation, these aims have largely decided the order in which particular industries have been nationalized. Basic industries, like coal-mining and electricity supply, whose policy and investment needs may affect the stability and progress of the whole economy, have come first. Liberating the consumer from private monopoly and possible exploitation has been another aim bringing "natural" monopolies such as electricity and gas supply into the nationalized fold, and later on will perhaps bring in man-created monopolies. These aims form part of the accepted ideals of equality and higher standards of

living. A further set of aims is however entailed in the Ministerial and Parliamentary supervision over the Public Corporation and the demand for periodical public inquiries. These aims refer not to economic efficiency, or consumer sovereignty and the satisfaction of individual wants, but to national interests and the needs of the community in health and amenities now and in the future. Indeed, with Britain's dependence on exports for its food supply, these aims refer to the nation's very survival. They look to economy and the proper distribution-for-use of national resources—natural and human. Once nationalized and having to consider price and output policies, State operated industries thus face the question whether they should satisfy national interests and human needs, or immediate individual consumer wants. The question may raise, and is today, raising dilemmas.

CHAPTER VII

STATE CONTROL OVER INDUSTRY

§1 Recapitulation and Finale

PREVIOUS chapters have set forth certain particular relations of the State to industry and to the parties constituting industry. They have shown how and why the State tries to defend labour from the employer, or consumer from monopolist; participates with labour and employer to avoid strikes and promote productivity; provides information about industry, services to industry and palliatives against the hazards of industry and takes on the direct operation of an industry. These activities involve the State either as a third party intervening between producing (and consuming) parties, or else as a direct provider of goods, services and money.

A wide range of State activities remain, however, where the State is neither a third or a first, but a second party—where the State faces industry or industries as integral wholes, not as a system of parties. The actual relation is expressed most simply as control *over* industry. The Oxford dictionary gives "to command" and "to hold in check" as main renderings of "to control". Both meanings must be borne in mind in considering State control over industry. "Holding in check" mainly takes the form of putting certain limits upon various lines of production, "command" of setting goals and targets *at* which industry should aim and of planning devices and steps *towards* these goals.

In many of the relations of the State to industry analysed hitherto, the State has merely stepped into the role of private organizations. In participating with employers and labour, in offering information services and palliatives, and in the direct operation of industry as described in Chapters IV, V and VI, the State is not exercising any unique types of power. It is engaged in activities open to private persons or bodies—conciliating, advising, exhorting, financing, insuring, managing, inducing—but which it can often perform with more weight and chance of success, within any one industry or, more particularly, for the economy as a whole. Official exhortation, for instance, to freeze wages and dividends or to check credit has met with some, though limited, success; a success certainly greater than any private exhortation would achieve. It is in the State's control over industry as in its defence of one industrial party from another, however, that its unique coercive powers come into play. This kit of tools, or armoury of weapons, as it may well be called, is so dangerous to individual liberty that special attention must be paid to those who wield it. After analysing the State's powers and tools for control this chapter includes therefore a section on the men and the organization of men behind the tools, before proceeding to consider the aims and achievement of the State control of industry. The final section reminds the reader of the wide variety of possible relations of the State to industry and consequently the wide variety of policies and devices the State can adopt to cope with problems or to attempt to achieve aims.

The verb "to cope" is used advisedly to remind readers that in periods of full employment and inflation, and shortage of man-power and of the means of international payments, much of the State's relation to industry is not the result of pursuing high aims set out beforehand, but of meeting, as democratically as possible, month-to-month crises threatening the very life of the nation. Current State policies and problems have nowhere been more tersely described than in the official memorandum, submitted in 1948 to the Organization for European Economic Co-operation on the Long Term Programme of the United Kingdom.[1] Though the acknowledged aim was no more ambitious than to "achieve and maintain a satisfactory level of economic activity without extraordinary outside assistance by 1952–53", planning was yet conditioned by "three fundamental facts":

"The economic fact that the United Kingdom economy must be heavily dependent upon international trade; the political fact that it is and intends to remain a democratic nation with a high degree of individual liberty; and the administrative fact that no economic

[1] H.M.S.O. Cmd. 7572, p. 1

planning body can be aware (or indeed ever could be aware) of more than the very general trends of future economic developments."

When a satisfactory level of activity is achieved, and within those fundamental conditions, State control may well become more constructive in pursuit of many aims beyond merely keeping the nation alive—along the lines, perhaps, of State action in the Development Areas soon to be described. In short, with the aid of its growing statistical and other information, already observed, State control may become effective positive planning in whatever direction is judged desirable.

§2 *Powers and Tools of State*

One use of the unique powers of coercion which the State alone can exercise, and regularly does exercise, is the "fiscal" control of taxation. Taxes are a compulsory payment which can be levied at an equal rate on all industries indiscriminately or, discriminately, on a particular industry or group of commodities.

Indiscriminate taxes falling on all industries include the profits taxes which may however discriminate between profits paid out in dividends and profits retained as reserves in the business. When investment is to be encouraged, present State policy is to tax distributed profits at a higher rate. The Royal Commission on Taxation of Profits and Income, however, recommended in 1955 against discrimination, since there was no virtue in promoting the mere retention of profits which might not actually be reinvested, and even if reinvested were likely to be invested in the originating industry, with less free choice than had new issues on the market. The allowances, free of tax, for depreciation or for new plant, may also be raised to encourage investment.

Taxes discriminate between industries in at least three ways. A tariff of import duties is imposed on particular products so as to favour certain home industries. Excise duties and purchase taxes are levied on products whether made at home or abroad, either to raise revenue or deliberately to check spending on certain industries, or both. And when levying taxes on profits, the allowances for depreciation or investment in new plant can discriminate in their degree of liberality between different industries.

The reverse side of taxation is expenditure, including the provision of grants or subsidies. Taxation allows a fund to be accumulated at the State's disposal which may be so disposed as to encourage certain industries rather than others. The central and local government subsidies on house building is the outstanding industrial example, but some of the subsidies on staple foods encouraged the food industries such as slaughtering, sugar-refining or baking, as well as agriculture.

This economic discrimination by the State, putting up burdens for some industries, diminishing them for others, is mainly effected by the Budget. Moreover the Budget may balance taxes and subsidies (together with other State expenditure); or it may allow for an overall surplus or a deficit thus forging an instrument for deflation or inflation which will affect industry, together with the general economy.

Another coercive power of the State over industry which it has, however, exercised less regularly than taxation, is compulsorily to put some limit upon physical quantities. The limit may be upon sales to consumers, by rationing, or by import quota or by allocation upon the total supply or distribution of raw materials, upon the supply of labour, or upon investment in plant, buildings and other capital goods. Furthermore, the State is enabled by licensing to limit the number of persons allowed to pursue certain industrial transactions or even to limit the transactions such as building to certain specific cases. These limiting, negative, "physical" controls (together with the State fixing of maximum prices which is unlikely to be effective in the long run without physical controls) have in Britain only been applied to industry in war-time or in the short-supply conditions of wars' aftermath. At present, over ten years after the end of the Second World War, physical controls are being reduced and since this book assumes conditions of peace, details perhaps, need not concern us.[1] Nevertheless, if State planning is to have any force, certain key controls must be retained.

Planning as contrasted with the market mechanism, has

[1]For the period 1945–50 *see* Gilbert Walker, *Economic Planning by Programme and Control*, 1957.

been defined as an acknowledgment of intentions (or aims) embodied in pre-arranged tasks based on knowledge of existing conditions and controlled or carried out by an organized structure.[1] To what extent and how the knowledge of existing conditions is acquired has already been discussed under the State's information services. The document, perhaps, of greatest importance in physical control is the annual Economic Survey, which sums up the international balance of payments position, and national income and expenditure at home. In 1947, the first year of its issue, the Economic Survey's "Conclusion" opens with the sentence, "In this Paper the Government has set out its conclusions on the economic state of the nation and has fixed targets and objectives for 1947".

These targets were not very far off actual past performances and the planned changes may be called marginal rather than radical. And in more recent years (e.g. in 1954) the conclusions offer no more than to "assess the prospects for the British economy during the next twelve months". Though acknowledging some aims and objectives and furnishing knowledge of existing conditions for the Government's own guidance, as well as the whole nation's, the Economic Survey can no longer be said to pre-arrange definite physical tasks even of a marginal order. It is now not much more than a part of the information and publicity activity of the State, together with a general declaration of ultimate aims—an activity important however in a democratic State where the collective organizations representing industrial parties must be up to date in their information and well oriented in their judgments, if they are usefully to participate in State government.

Though specific targets are not now published beforehand on paper, departments of State have physical quantities in mind as tending towards certain national aims which will be considered in detail later. The quantities involved for industry are amounts of goods of various kinds to be provided in a given place or time from a certain distribution of resources and factors of production. State planning is undertaken when it is thought that the market mechanism, catering as it does for private demands, not necessarily national needs, will, if let alone, not

[1]Florence, *Logic of British and American Industry*, 1953, p. 267.

provide the needed quantities by the required distribution of resources.

Needs and resources are set out against one another in economic programmes or "budgets". The term budget was applied to physical control in the first Economic Survey where it was noted that, unlike the National Budget, the items are not originally set against one another in terms of money but in terms of man-years of work and quantities of goods. Yet like the National Budget these economic budgets bring sources of income and expenditure together, estimate for the future, and are administratively useful in giving each of the chief departments or offices, on whom responsibility is delegated, a total of money, man-power or physical quantities *within* which they may have discretion.

The budgets that continue of greatest importance to State planning and control are budgets of man-power, of raw material including imports, and of capital investment.

During the war, the *man-power budget* was found an instrument of the greatest use in physical planning and control. Areas where resources in labour were inadequate to needs were labelled scarlet, labour was directed into them (particularly from the "green" areas of labour superfluity) and additional industrial activity as far as possible kept out. Scarlet areas still exist today, where jobs far outnumber available workers but the State has had to give up its control over man-power.

The Trade Unions, exemplifying the continuance of *laissez-faire* philosophy, neither accept a national wages policy (whereby the State determines the structure of differential wages in accordance with resources in labour and the national requirements of different occupations) nor allow the continuance of the war-time coercive (as an alternative to the economic sanction) of the direction of labour. The Trades Union Congress protested when, in February 1948, the Labour Government issued, as a White Paper, its *Statement on Personal Incomes, Cost and Prices*, which declared that any claim for increases in income "must be considered on its national merits, not on the basis of maintaining a former relativity between different occupations and industries".[1] The Trade Unions, indeed, appear to prefer the

[1]Flanders, *Trade Unions*, 1952. Hutchinson's University Library, p. 110.

possibly coercive direction of individual members, to any State interference with their prerogative of bargaining on wages. They agreed to the Control of Engagements Order during the war, and again to its reimposition (in theory) in August 1947. In practice, little use was made of the post-war government powers and the order was withdrawn in March 1950.

With full employment, labour is the factor in shortest supply. The golden rule of all planning, as Professor Robinson remarks, "is that it must be done in terms of the scarcest of resources".[1] So this opposition to any State control and man-power policy severely handicaps planning. State government must fall back on budgets for resources more under control than labour: budgets for imported materials, and for capital.

Since 1939 a gap has yawned between the total value of imports and exports, visible and invisible, owing to more liabilities abroad, to loss of interest from overseas investments, sold to finance the war, and to worsening "terms of trade"—the cost of goods imported rising faster than the prices of goods exported. The shortage of the means of paying for imports is likely to continue and justifies State interference since, in place of materials of high national priority, the market mechanism would pick out for importation materials of high profitability. A programme of material imports either through direct State bulk-buying of the material or through physical control of market buying is, in short, important while means of international payment, particularly in hard currencies like dollars, run short. For national viability, as argued later, materials for exporting and capital forming industries must have priority over material for home-consumed luxuries.

More important still to the structure of industry is *control over capital investment*. Industry is becoming more and more capitalized and thus more sensitive to State investment policy, whether through nationalization (where, as we have seen, the need for capital is often a prime consideration) or through control. Investment control, too, is probably less injurious to personal liberty than control over the other factors of production, such as labour or even the expropriation of specific pieces of land. If the State is really to plan industry in a society remaining free,

[1]*Lessons of the British War Economy*, Ed. Chester, 1951, p. 57.

the physical control of investment is likely to be a most powerful tool.

It must first be observed that taxation, particularly progressive taxation, must reduce the capacity to save while high Bank and other interest rates reduce the willingness to lay money out on equipment. Within this boundary, however, State encouragement and control, by limiting projects of low national priority and selecting those of high priority can occur at each of the three stages in the investment of capital—saving, financing and outlay on physical equipment and building.[1] The State encourages saving by exhortation and savings campaigns, and by issuing saving certificates and other "safe" fixed interest stock (though not safe against inflation), and forcibly reduces private spending by direct taxation; it controls new financial issues on the market through the Capital Issues Committee created by the Borrowing (Control and Guarantees) Act of 1946; and until recently, at least, it controlled and selected outlay on equipment by its prohibition of factory building without a licence and by its allocation of timber and steel and supply of machines and other engineering products. The three stages of investment are not always subject to a division of labour, however. When a company reinvests its profits in plant, its Board of Directors is saving by limiting dividends, is equipping its factories and financing the equipment all in one. Here the State can still, however, control saving and finance by differential taxation of distributed and retained profits, by varying tax allowances on equipment and by the controls over outlay upon equipment.

Illustrations of the devices and difficulties involved in various forms of control will occur as we discuss (in §3 and §4) the men in charge, and the aims of planning and control. Before proceeding, however, attention must be drawn to certain consequences inherent in physical and price control.

(i) Control is wasteful of administrative man-power—a waste roughly indicated by the growth since 1934 of the civil service departments dealing with industry, without corresponding offset in reduction of staff of private organizations. Indeed, private business must often add to its staff persons specially detailed for coping with State officials; and people, like the notorious

---

[1]Florence, *Logic of British and American Industry*, 1953, pp. 282–3.

Mr. Stanley, investigated by the Linskey tribunal, may set up as "contact-men" or "intermediaries" between those staffs and the government officials.

(ii) Controls will frustrate and even take the place of that personal initiative which Mill (see pp. 37-8) thought so important in society. In the reaction against *laissez-faire* since Mill's time, the *entrepreneur* activities were taken for granted as expendable and it was assumed that control over the *entrepreneur*, including taxation as well as the defence of various parties from the *entrepreneur*, could be carried out indefinitely. With the acknowledgment of the need for efficient and enterprising management, however, second thoughts are arising and leading to psychological and sociological inquiry similar to that applied to the industrial worker. Managers, apparently, like being frustrated and by-passed no more than labour. To have a new building, a factory owner had, until recently, to satisfy the local authority as to the site, the Board of Trade on the location, the Ministry of Works on starting dates, and he was liable, on an "investment cut", to indefinite postponement after all officials had been satisfied. If frustration is carried too far managers will, like labour in some jobs, either restrict activities or leave their occupation and there will be little hope of their effective replacement.

(iii) If the whole economy is not to be planned and controlled, as it is in a totalitarian system, the excepted unplanned parts are likely to flourish at the expense of the planned part. Factories will, for instance, cease to make goods whose price is controlled, and will turn to uncontrolled goods where they can get larger profits. Alternatively producers may contrive to make the controlled goods, but sell them at illegal prices on a "black" market with consequent encouragement of "spivs", as well as the "intermediaries".

All the same, it remains an attractive proposal that certain standard products (like the Utility goods of the last war, though of better design and quality) should be mass-produced at a low cost, and consequently a low price for a wide market. If the State is to implement such a proposal, however, a strong mixture of coercive control must be used. Production by firms of a certain proportion of standard goods will have to be made a condition for devoting the rest of their capacity to uncontrolled goods.

F°

(iv) Physical controls are not as sensitive to changes in the economic situation as prices on the market. The degree of insensitivity will depend on the human controllers to be considered shortly, but generally they must, by their very position, be remote from the events of the market and, if the controllers originated the scheme of control which they are working, they are liable to cling to it as their child. In 1948, indeed, the government felt the need to appoint "examiners of controls" to consider the mending and ending of controls dispassionately.

These consequences, general to controls, certainly throw the onus of proof on the policy of maintaining controls. But there seems no alternative to physical controls where necessary resources continue to be in short supply and where the uncontrolled market mechanism would not result in the required distribution of resources among national needs. This situation still (1956) holds in Britain for investment, for the balance of payment in dollars, and for necessary imports whose price it is not policy to increase by the economic disincentive of tariffs.

§3 *The Men behind the Tools*

The distinctive feature of overall control and planning is the intention to promote the public interest by the visible hand of the State, rather than by Adam Smith's invisible hand of the market mechanism. The coercive, incentive and hortative procedures of the State cannot therefore be considered in isolation from the hands using these instruments. At the centre lies a certain "corpus" of civil servants; but in industrial matters the most remarkable development is that British governments have in recent years (and particularly during the world wars and their aftermath) been so anxious to consult representatives of the industrial parties concerned.

Much of the detailed participation of the State with particular industries has already been discussed in Chapter V; for industry as a whole the important consultative bodies are the National Production Advisory Council for Industry (N.P.A.C.I.) and the Ministry of Labour's National Joint Advisory Council (N.J.A.C.). The latter council, composed of representatives of the British Employers' Federation, the Trades Union Congress and the nationalized industries, advises on wages policies and relations between employers and workers. The N.P.A.C.I. is precluded from discussing these topics, but otherwise views the whole economy. It is composed of representatives of nationalized industries and private industrialists, and of the Trade Union Council, together with senior civil servants, and—by including their chairman—forms the central keystone of the structure of the Regional Boards for Industry. On these Regional Boards employers and Trade Unions are represented and all the government departments likely to be interested in local industrial developments, and particularly in policies of State control.

The Regional Boards' discussions range over such matters as local shortages of labour or materials, export programmes, effect of purchase tax on employment; and it is through these Boards that industrial enterprises get their licences and allocation for investment projects. To build a factory, for instance, a firm must first apply to the regional office of the appropriate government department. The staff of this office will then examine the project on the score of its likely efficiency, its possibilities for export, sources of labour and suitability and location generally. Many of these considerations involve a number of different State departments: rural dispersion of industry, for instance, the Board of Trade, the Board of Agriculture, the Ministry of Works. The Regional Board thus forms a convenient meeting ground for the exchange of views between industry and the relevant State authorities and also serves to relieve the central State machinery. It is a device both for joint consultation and for the devolution of responsibility.

Consultation with industry takes place not only in administering industrial policy, but also in the original framing of policy and communicating contemplated policy. Advisory bodies from industry are, in short, part of the legislative and planning as well as the executive process. In 1947 the Economic Planning Board was set up "to advise His Majesty's Government on the best use of our economic resources, both for the realization of a long-term plan and for remedial measures against our immediate difficulties". The Board is composed of three employers and three Trade Unionists, the Permanent Secretaries of the Government Departments chiefly concerned and expert members of the staff of the Chief Planning Officer and the Director of the Economic

Section of the Cabinet Office. The Economic Planning Board thus combines in its personnel the powers of a general staff and a consultative two-way channel of communication with the two sides of industry—a channel supplementary to the direct communication of the Trades Union Congress or the Federation of British Industries with the government.

Writing as early as 1921 Delisle Burns[1] pointed out that the State had looked to Employers' Associations and Federations "when there had been any attempt to organize what are called the relations of employer and employed", and that "without Trade Unions the present governmental treatment of industry would be impossible". He proceeds "not only does the State recognize Trade Unions, but they actually form part of governmental organization". This devolution of State powers both for devising legislation and (for example the Wages Boards, pp. 55-9 above) administering it has gone far since 1921, even as far as letting industries "plan by consent" for themselves how to allocate supplies among their members or customers.

Deliberation with industry and partial devolution of decision upon its representatives have been facilitated by the habit of the Civil Service to make decisions by means of interdepartmental deliberation. The industrial representatives can be added to the civil servants who would in any case have formed a committee, or at least would have consulted with colleagues from different departments, either face to face or by interchange of memoranda. Final responsibility to Parliament is pinned upon the Minister, and the civil servants who advise him and whom he consults remain anonymous. The theory behind the committee or consultation is that wiser and fairer decisions are reached if the adviser or consultant merges his personality in a discussion between different minds with different loyalties and experiences looking round at the different interests likely to be involved. Industrial pressure groups from separate industries or from labour or employers as a whole form to push their particular interests upon the government. But advisory committees bring matters "over the counter" and help to ensure that similar cases, though with differing degrees of pressure applied, are similarly treated and the public interest considered. The drawback is that

[1]*Government and Industry*, 1921, pp. 71 and 74.

such discussion and circumspection will be lengthy (if departmental vested interests and empire building are involved, often interminably lengthy) and will appear to be tied up in red tape, and the final decision, if and when it comes through, bureaucratic.

Where discussion is of the essence of the State's relation to industry, as in negotiation with labour and employers to settle a dispute or in preparation of legislation to defend one industrial party from another, the circumspect attitude of the Civil Service is fit for its purpose.

But it is unsuitable where the State is directly engaged in the operation or even in the control of industry with its continually changing problems, and where rapidity of decision may be essential in seizing an opportunity or coping with a crisis. The abandonment has already been noted of organization by department of State for operating industries other than the Post Office.

Apart from their tradition of circumspection and deliberation the education and selection of civil servants for specific activities does not make for quick decision. This is particularly evident in the State's relations to industry, undreamed of when the Civil Service traditions were formed. The officials in control over industry are not experts in economics or organization, let alone industrial organization; the Civil Service, on the contrary, holds the anti-expert theory that a good brain selected by a stiff examination in the classics, history, mathematics and/or other general subjects is enough. The government departments related to industry must, like other departments, accept their staff from the Civil Service Commission without regard to special aptitude or knowledge. This theory means that each economic problem, as it arises, tends to be argued with colleagues from first principles, sometimes without apprehension either of industrial structure or of the apparatus of thought built up by economists.

The Civil Service is deliberate and circumspect in making decisions, and the members involved in making decisions not expert or knowledgeable in the economic or industrial issues. Nevertheless, by their sheer mental ability, incorruptibility and resistance to pressure groups, and consistency of outlook and politics, Civil Servants will exercise a profound influence on the State's industrial policy whether policy appears in legislation largely prepared through discussion with them, or in the orders they issue directly. The influence of the Civil Service in industrial affairs will probably be thrown on the side of coherence, conservation and the administratively convenient rather than of immediate fulfilment of popular (or sectional) wants or even the immediate realistic adjustment to a crisis.

§4 *Aims and Achievements of Control*

The State has certain instruments for control over industry and certain aims imposed by public opinion, for which, failing the market mechanism, the State must take responsibility. How are these aims achieved, or at least attempted by the instruments of control?

Some aims lying outside industry and the economy that are referred to State action involve the defence of one party in industry against another and have been attempted by procedures described in Chapter IV: health by Factory Acts; minimum standards of living by Wages Boards; and many economic and industrial aims such as greater efficiency and progress and industrial peace, by the procedure (described in Chapter V) of State participation with industry. Other economic and industrial aims require however that general control over industry and the factors of production, land, labour and especially investment, which has just been described.

In the heyday of the *laissez-faire* doctrine the use of some minimum machinery of general State control over the economy was accepted in order to ensure financial stability. Today, when wide deviations from *laissez-faire* are warranted by a wide variety of aims, those attempted by the procedures of overall control, are mainly (*a*) the maintenance of high and stable employment; (*b*) economic viability for the nation as a whole and aggregate provision for an acceptable average standard of living; (*c*) economic equality and the provision of fair (or at least fairer) shares to all. One aim may, of course, get in the way of another. Full employment, has, since 1945, for instance tended towards instability in the form of inflation and provision for education, health and amenities may, in the short run at least, get in the way of national viability and the general material standard of living. Clearly such conflict cannot be left for the market mechanism to resolve, and State interference is more justified perhaps than ever.

(*a*) Full or (as it is officially defined in the White Paper of 1944) "high and stable" employment has been found to require two lines of policy. The unemployment of the inter-war years which shocked public opinion into demanding State action was a compound of time and space elements: a period of slump and depression from which industry, unaided by the State, found it hard to recover quickly; and certain depressed areas into which industry unaided by the State found it hard to move. The State procedure for coping with both elements, strongly influenced by Keynes, was adumbrated in the White Paper of 1944. The fall in private investment associated with periods of increased unemployment was to be offset by an increase in public investment in directions planned beforehand. Partly to finance this, the central government budget was to be allowed to fall into deficit. With the advent of the Labour Government in 1945 no doubt budgetary deficits would have been planned and public works undertaken; but with continued full employment, without such aid by the State, the occasion did not arise.

The procedure to cope with local unemployment in depressed areas, on the other hand, was put into effect through the Distribution of Industry Act setting up Development Areas. The key to the situation is that certain of the unemployment-prone industries making capital goods had tended to be localized in certain areas, notably iron and steel smelting and rolling, and coal mining on the English north-east coast, the Clyde area of Scotland, and South Wales, and on the Clyde and the north-east coast ship-building also. In consequence, the general incidence of unemployment in the regions including these areas towered above the unemployment rate for other regions and the country as a whole. In August 1932, at the depth of the Great Depression, the unemployment rate was 27·9 per cent for Scotland, 30·9 per cent for the north-east coast and 39·1 per cent for Wales, as against 23·1 per cent for the whole country.[1] A further disadvantage of these localized industries from the standpoint of family standards of living was that they provided no occupations for women.

[1]Fuller details are given in Florence, *Labour*, Hutchinson's University Library, 1949, pp. 156–63.

Family poverty due to the unemployment of the menfolk was, by the "unoccupation" of the women, left unrelieved. State policy for the prevention of unemployment in the depressed areas was thus to introduce industries less subject to cyclical depression and especially industries giving occupation to women.

This policy of industrial diversification was attempted by the Commissioner of the Special Areas (appointed early in 1936) mainly through exhortation and some financial assistance, particularly in providing sites and buildings on Trading Estates. The policy was accepted by the (Barlow) Royal Commission on the Distribution of the Industrial Population in its recommendation (para. 428) of:

"Encouragement of a reasonable balance of industrial development, so far as possible, throughout the various divisions or regions of Great Britain, coupled with appropriate diversification of industry in each division or region throughout the country."

The Royal Commission also wished to prevent the establishment of further industry in "congested" areas. For this purpose New Towns with their own industries have, since the war, been set up, most of them in a ring at distances of about thirty miles from London; and diversification in the depressed, now "development", areas combined with "decongestion" by moving the diversifying industries from the congested areas.

During the war the State had a powerful instrument at its disposal owing to the enlargement of the activities described in the last chapter of trading *in*, and operation *of*, industries. The State gave priority in war contracts to factories in the depressed areas and built there a number of Royal Ordnance Factories which after the war were leased or sold on liberal terms to private enterprise. Immediate availability of premises is always an important factor in the location of plants and never more so than in the pent-up boom after a war.

Exhortation, the chief incentive before the war, was not so completely relied upon afterwards. Instead, the State undertook perhaps the most thorough piece of positive planning attempted in Britain. The negative tools of prohibition and refusal of physical allocation were used in conjunction with affirmative

State building and subsidies. Under the Distribution of Industry Act of 1945 all proposed industrial building had to be notified to the Board of Trade and building was encouraged in the "Development Areas", as the "depressed" and "special" areas were duly called. State "encouragement" took the form of refusals of licences to build—and refusals of allocations of steel and timber to build with—in the congested areas, but offers of land, buildings and trading estate facilities at subsidized prices to those moving into the Development Areas.

Some industries, however, are rooted to the place where their raw materials are extracted; others are tied to the place where their consumers reside; others linked to a complex of interdependent industries. For all these industries location cannot, economically speaking, be planned at the will of the State. Other industries though "footloose" and manoeuvrable do not employ women or are not as stable as required in the Development Areas. In short, State policy in its aim of decongestion and diversification required an analysis of the characteristics of each industry. Among expanding firms, willing to build plants in Development Areas, certain ranges of industries may not be frequent and analytical selection an ideal only partially attainable.

Clothing is an outstanding instance of a footloose industry, encouraged to build because of its relative stability and its employment of women and location in cities. In 1939 clothing workers formed 4·2 per cent of all workers over the country as a whole, but only 0·9 per cent and 1·5 per cent of all workers in the South Wales and north-east coast development areas. By 1951 the overall national percentage of clothing workers had fallen to 3·2 per cent but in the two areas had risen to 2·1 and 2·8 per cent. Thus the Development Areas were gradually getting their share of some industries employing women—and employing them, in the past, largely in congested cities.

To assess achievement in raising employment generally, comparative statistics can be given only for a whole region, not for the precise Development Areas. In any case, a final test can be applied only when statistics of local incomes are available. But it is significant that in Wales in 1931–36 the average rate of unemployment at 32·7 per cent was 15 points above the national level for Great Britain, whereas in 1952–54 at 2·6 per cent it was only 1·1 above. In the Scottish region, also including a large Development area, a fall of the unemployment rate in the same period from 23·9 per cent to 3·1 per cent meant a reduction in the differential of unemployment rates from 6·1 to 1·6. Northern Ireland, with an average for 1952–54 of 8·2 per cent, is indeed the only region of the United Kingdom where unemployment remains higher than the rate of 3 per cent which Lord Beveridge considered a practicable level of full employment.

The deviation of Northern Ireland from the full employment pattern in other regions demonstrates the limits of State planning in a free society. No firm is coerced to place its factories in any region or area, and firms seem to have considered Northern Ireland too out of the way and inaccessible from the rest of the British economy. State-planned location of factories in the other areas formerly depressed does not seem to have raised costs unduly. Some research comparing the same firm's branches in Birmingham with newer branches opened up with State help in South Wales seemed to show only a slightly increased cost and this cost was probably outweighed by the fact that the acute shortage of labour in Birmingham might have made increased production there, except at prohibitive cost, impossible.

Instead of bringing factories to the labour supply the *laissez-faire* alternative to State development would have been to let labour ("stimulated" by the unemployment and semi-starvation on the dole at home) move to the factories carrying on elsewhere. In the absence of sufficient new houses "elsewhere", this transference of labour would at best be a slow and painful process, but even if the migrants were satisfactorily housed much capital would be wasted in the houses, streets, schools, drains and other public utilities left behind. Considerable emigration from depressed industrial areas did in fact take place. The Administrative County of Glamorganshire, for instance, had lost 3·9 per cent of its 1931 population by 1951, and County Durham 2 per cent, while England and Wales as a whole increased by 9·5 per cent. Thus the *laissez-faire* and the State development solutions were not incompatible, and both were at work to reduce regional unemployment. But without State interference, which, incidentally, included payment of some of the cost of labour transference and migration, the response of the supply of labour to the demand would have been slower and less complete.

(b) The general rise in unemployment expected after the war did not take place. Instead the rate kept as low as 1½ per cent in 1946 and 1947. Except for the procedure adopted in the Development Areas and in keeping the general rate of interest low, none of the State plans for raising public and private demand, were brought into action. It gradually became clear to the Government that it was not low and unstable employment that had to be checked, but, in the interests of national viability, boom conditions and inflation.

Viability is defined as the capacity of maintaining life. When post-war economic problems were found not to be different but much the same as those of the war-time siege economy, the besieged had to be found not *any* sort of work but work essential to national existence. Since Britain cannot feed herself from her own agricultural resources, the essential work was to manufacture exports to pay for imported food and necessary raw materials or to produce substitutes for imports, or both. Similarity to a siege economy was made still more evident by the cold war and in particular the rearmament and restocking programme following the communist *coup d'état* in Czechoslovakia in 1948 and aggression in Korea in 1950.

Uncontrolled by the State, industries would not necessarily aim at sufficient munitions of war or exports, since products were easy to sell in the private consumers' home market, and foreign markets were more troublesome to conquer. State interference was thus justified in the interest of national viability, meaning literally the capacity to maintain minimum standards of living.

Interference in industry took the form mainly of the physical and economic controls already described. Imports were limited by quota or licence, exports encouraged by allocation of raw materials, of equipment and of building licences to firms or plants exporting goods, and for the period already mentioned direction of labour was reimposed in order to compel mobility towards exporting and other essential industries. Further to check home demand and reduce consumption almost to war-time austerity, budget surpluses were planned, particularly during the Chancellorship of Sir Stafford Cripps, by means of increased excise and purchase taxes on consumers' luxury goods.

Producers' goods present more difficult problems in a policy for viability. In the final stage of the investment process, when finance is used in outlay on equipment, wages and salaries are paid out, but no additional consumer goods appear on the market to mop up the additional purchasing power. The result of more money chasing no more goods is inflation. For this reason restraint and a general cut in investment have been urged. On the other hand the new machines and plant in which industry invests are likely to be more efficient than the old and to produce goods at lower cost. Limitation of investment will thus handicap the home as against the foreign producer and tend to reduce exports and increase (the lower-cost) imports from countries where investment has not been controlled.

(c) In addition to the aim of high general employment (with employment as high as possible in every region) and to the struggle to keep the national economy viable, State control over industry is also applied to help the State activities, described in an earlier chapter, towards achieving more equal distribution of incomes.

The risk to viability has been partly caused, however, through this very attempt to equalize distribution by raising the real minimum standard of living, especially when, with price inflation, the money minimum has continually to be raised to keep the real standard stationary. Till viability is more assured therefore State control and probably other State activities aiming at greater (real) equality are not likely to be developed very much further. But development has already gone far.

Many measures for more equal distribution enforced in the programme of the Welfare State, such as the free National Medical Service or Health Insurance, are not primarily industrial, but others involve State control over industry, including limitation and encouragement of one line of production rather than another. Rationing by (equally distributed) card and not by (unequally distributed) cash, when food and clothing is scarce, is a leading case of limitation; another is the requirement of a licence for building houses and extensions to houses of more than a certain value. On the other hand, the housing of the poorer members of the community has been encouraged by central and local government subsidies and although the central government's general subsidization of comparatively low-rent housing is gradually being abandoned, building for the very poorest householders is still to be encouraged by subsidies for slum-clearance and redevelopment. Subsidies were also paid for the standard foods, including flour, bread, sugar, meat and bacon, forming a high proportion of the expenditure of poorer families. The total food subsidy, reaching in 1949 almost £500 million but subsequently reduced, was a tool as powerful as the free medical service and the palliative by insurance in raising minimum standards of living. The subsidies also aimed at increasing total food production at home, even at a higher cost, and may sometimes have increased prices. The State thus intervenes by various controls and coercive procedures to increase the consumption, or at least the production, of the goods catering to the needs of the poorer sections of the community. Progressive income taxes and death duties redistribute still further the volume of demand for different industrial products.

Seebohm Rowntree made surveys of poverty in his native city of York in 1899, 1936 and 1950 and it is possible roughly to estimate the achievement of some of the State policies in their aim of raising the minimum modes of living. Between 1899 and 1936 when wages boards, national insurance and pensions were being introduced, the percentage of all families whose income was below that necessary for bare subsistence had dropped from 15·5 to 6·8 per cent. This insufficiency was due to low wages for 8 per cent of all families in 1899, but only for 0·6 per cent in 1936. Between 1936 and 1950 Rowntree used as his poverty line a higher standard than bare subsistence. Individuals whose income was below this standard fell from 14·2 to 0·37 per cent of all individuals surveyed, a change due mainly to a composite of full employment, family allowances and food subsidies. Rowntree attempts to assess the effect of food subsidies alone. Had they not been introduced he calculated the percentage below the poverty line would have been 2·42 per cent instead of 0·37 per cent.[1]

[1]Rowntree and Lavers, *Poverty and the Welfare State*, 1951, pp. 37–45.

The major aims of State control over industry: high and stable employment, national viability, and more equal distribution of income may be summed up in the words of a Government White Paper "to improve the standard of living of the people". But there appears to be some minor aims in the State control over industry which may be brought under the title of amenities.

One form of physical control by the State was approved very early by leading economists—the control of land for town-planning. One factory, noisy, or polluting streams, or emitting smoke, smells, dust or noxious fumes, could ruin the amenities of a whole residential neighbourhood or recreational green belt and legislation as early as the Town Planning Act of 1909 or, later, the Interim Development Act of 1943 allowed local authorities to limit the building of factories to certain zones within their boundaries. Even in areas where factories were allowed, legislation, such as the Public Health Acts of 1875, 1926 and 1936, enabled local authorities to have control over smoke and to make factories good neighbours. Under this legislation the smoke had to be proved noxious to health, and State action for smoke abatement has hitherto not been very effective. It is only recently that local authorities have been enabled to plan and control smokeless zones, within which the burning of all smoky fuels by households as well as industry is prohibited.

Factory smoke is perhaps the leading case (and so cited by Professor Pigou as a matter of growing importance) of the divergences between social and trade net product. Private trade gains little, or thinks to gain little, by abating smoke; but society gains much in avoiding loss "in respect of health, of injury to buildings and vegetables, of expenses of washing clothes and cleaning rooms, of expenses for the provision of extra artificial light".[1]

If "standard of living" is interpreted widely enough (and with rising material standards the uses of education and leisure get increasingly appreciated) amenities may be counted as part of the standard. It follows that some private "trading" product and efficiency might be sacrificed in favour of public "social" product.

[1] *Wealth and Welfare*, 1912, p. 159.

In 1948 when discussing public policy on the size of industrial plants I put forward an argument capable of general application.[1]

"If the differences in output from the alternative methods of organization were not great, a difference in the social desirability of the small-plant or of the large-plant method might, in determining policy, be taken as overriding economic efficiency. But if the efficiency of the two methods were *not* tolerably similar, then efficiency would, except for exceptional circumstances, have to hold sway. Though relative efficiency should not dictate industrial policy it should clearly be given weight in a compromise, and its precise weight should, if possible, be known. The cost should be counted. Otherwise resources in brawn, brain and gear will be wasted."

Applied to amenity the argument would run that other things such as efficiency being equal, or *not very unequal*, industry should be controlled to allow the citizen greater enjoyment of his living, as well as his working conditions.

§5 *Control and Totality of State Action*

State control over industry is clearly a procedure used for all the main aims of State activity. These aims may be summed up as of four types—in ascending order of industrial implication: health, safety and amenity; equality and democracy, including consumer sovereignty; stability of the economy and security of the individual; efficiency, progress and viability of the whole economy, including defence of the nation. State control over industry, however, is only one procedure among the others which have been analysed in earlier chapters with the same types of aim. Health, safety and amenity were the aims of the Factory Act defence of the worker from his employer, and of State participation with worker and employer in joint councils. More equal distribution of incomes was the aim of the Wages Council form of defence from the employer; democracy (or consumer sovereignty) one of the aims of the Company Law and the Monopoly Commission form of defence from directors and monopolists, of the State's publication of information about industry and of State operation of industry. Stability and security was an aim of State operation of industry and of

[1]*Investment, Location and Size of Plant*, 1948, pp. 122–3.

palliatives against industrial hazards. Efficiency, progress and economic viability was one of the aims of the State's participation in sponsoring Development Councils and of State services for industry and operation of industries.

The State, in short, has for its various aims a large totality of tools. If one set of tools fails to achieve a given aim others can be tried; a government should not pin its faith to any one set such as say tariffs or nationalization. The art of State government is to a considerable extent that of considering all the various tools available and finally deciding which tools to use—what procedures to apply—for the various aims public opinion judges of value.

National viability is the fundamental condition—a condition without which the other aims would be either impossible or become stability and equality of misery—and is less a matter of value-judgment and more of expert administration, economic and technological logistics. The pursuit of all aims, however, involve questions of the relative efficiency of alternative procedures—questions of means to which the social sciences can help to find answers. State administrators are usually given aims embodied in certain fairly precise targets, say the annual building of 300,000 houses for workers. Their task is to think out devices and compute the economic, political, and psychological incentives or coercives of various strengths, that are required to hit the target without hindering the hitting of some other given target—say the extension of factories making for a certain increase in exports, or, in spite of higher demands, less overtime for workers, or a lower price for building materials.

State policies may not only conflict one with another and require expert co-ordination but must take account of the underlying economic and social forces. Devices and computation must consider what industrial trends are occurring in directions away from those required by the aims, and in particular whether these trends are ultimately self-rectifying or cumulative "vicious circles". Short-term unemployment due to mobility and transfer from one industry to another in response to changes in demand is, for instance, in a different category from long-term unemployment as a result of which the worker loses his health and efficiency and consequently his fitness for employment generally—unemployment circling viciously into unemployment. It is indeed the vicious circles—the social chain-reaction of the market mechanism let alone—which State policy must in particular get information about and control over, and from which it must defend society. In controlling and planning industry one aim of a free society must, however, not be forgotten: the aim of letting its members remain as free of State coercion or interference as possible. This value-judgment appears to be as strongly held by British public opinion today as a hundred years ago, and it is in consequence of this judgment that any new intervention of the State must rationally be justified. This book has tried to show that such justification is possible for many forms and directions of State action unheard of last century—but the need for explicit justification remains.

BOOKS FOR FURTHER READING[1]

1. OFFICIAL DOCUMENTS AND PERIODICALS
   Ministry of Labour, *Annual Reports*
   Ministry of Labour, *Labour Gazette* (Monthly)
   Ministry of Labour, *Industrial Relations Handbook*
   Board of Trade Journal (Weekly)
   Annual Reports of the Chief Inspector of Factories
   Annual Reports of Public Corporations in Nationalized Industries
   Annual Reports by Board of Trade on Monopolies and Restrictive Practices
   Reports of the Monopolies and Restrictive Practices Commission
   Report of the (Barlow) Royal Commission on the *Distribution of the Industrial Population*, 1940
   Report of the (Cohen) Committee on *Company Law Amendment* 1945. Cmd. 6659
   Report of the (Ridley) Committee on *National Policy for the Use of Fuel and Power Resources*, 1950. Cmd. 8647
   Report of the (Herbert) Committee of Inquiry into the *Electricity Supply Industry*, 1956.
   Acts of Parliament
   Parliamentary Debates, *Hansard*

2. LABOUR PROBLEMS
   R. H. Tawney. *Minimum Rates in the Tailoring Industry*, 1915
   F. Tillyard. *The Worker and the State*, 1923
   E. M. Burns. *Wages and the State*, 1926
   A. G. B. Fisher. *Some Problems of Wages and their Regulation in Great Britain since* 1918, 1926
   Lord Amulree. *Industrial Arbitration*, 1929
   H. Clay. *The Problem of Industrial Relations*, 1929

[1]"Classics" influencing Public Opinion are given in Table 1, p. 20-1.

P. S. Florence. *Labour,* 1949
A. Flanders. *Trade Unions,* 1952
G. D. H. Cole. *An Introduction to Trade Unionism,* 1953
B. Wootton. *The Social Foundations of Wage Policy,* 1955

3. THE STATE AND INDUSTRIAL ENTERPRISE
   D. Burns. *Government and Industry,* 1921
   Ed. D. N. Chester. *Lessons of the British War Economy,* 1951
   P. E. P. *Government and Industry,* 1951
   Gilbert Walker. *Economic Planning by Programme and Control,* 1957

4. INDUSTRIAL BACKGROUND AND NATIONALIZED INDUSTRIES
   J. A. Hobson. *The Evolution of Capitalism,* 1917
   B. W. Lewis. *British Planning and Nationalization,* 1952
   Ed. Robson. *Problems of Nationalized Industry,* 1952
   Clegg and Chester. *The Future of Nationalization,* 1953
   P. S. Florence. *Logic of British and American Industry,* 1953

INDEX

For Product Safety Concerns and Information please contact our EU
representative GPSR@taylorandfrancis.com Taylor & Francis Verlag GmbH,
Kaufingerstraße 24, 80331 München, Germany

Printed and bound by CPI Group (UK) Ltd, Croydon, CR0 4YY
08/05/2025
01864411-0001